THE RESONANCE OF TRUTH AND UNITY

A GUIDE TO SELF-REALIZATION AND HIGHER CONSCIOUSNESS

BABA TYSON

ISBN: 979-8-9941208-0-4

Published by Truth & Unity Press

The practices in this book are shared from personal experience and are offered for educational and exploratory purposes only. They are not medical advice. If you have any cardiovascular, respiratory, neurological, psychological, or other medical conditions, consult a qualified healthcare professional before experimenting with breath retention or any altered breathing practices. Never practice breath retention while driving, swimming, or operating machinery. Proceed with awareness and personal responsibility.

TRANSMITTED IN

Arambol, Goa, India

October 2025

For you,
the one who is ready to remember.
For the one who has faced fear
and still chosen love.
May these words guide you
home to yourself.

CONTENTS

OPENING TRANSMISSION

This isn't a book you read with your mind. It's a transmission you feel with your heart. Every word carries a frequency meant to remind you of what you already are, the awareness experiencing itself through this moment.

Nothing here is meant to convince you or give you something new to believe. It's simply here to help you remember what's always been true. *The Resonance of Truth and Unity* is a living reflection of Consciousness remembering itself through you. It's an invitation to raise your frequency, dissolve fear, and live as the awareness in the ever-expanding now.

Each transmission builds upon the last, guiding you deeper into the direct experience of what you already are. Every word is vibration. What begins as reading opens into feeling.

PREFACE

My life changed in a single moment of remembrance.

What began as a personal awakening unfolded into a living transmission, a reflection of how Consciousness remembers itself through the human experience.

In these pages, I share what I've realized firsthand through direct experience. Every circumstance, every challenge, and every reflection has guided me deeper into the remembrance of who and what we truly are. These insights continue to expand, because awakening isn't a destination. It's an ever-unfolding remembrance of awareness itself.

Everyone I've shared this with who's remained open and willing to apply the process to the best of their ability has experienced transformation on some level. That's because this isn't a belief system or a self-help technique. It's how the very structure of reality operates. You don't have to believe me. Try it for yourself and see what happens.

It's an honor and a privilege to share this experience with you. You're free to test it in your own experience and share it with others who are ready. The more people who raise their frequency, the more the collective Consciousness evolves toward unity.

A NOTE BEFORE YOU BEGIN

Beloved one, before you begin, I want to share something important.

This isn't a book to be rushed through or casually read. It's a transmission. The words you're about to read carry a frequency. Each sentence holds an energy that can only be felt in stillness. So take your time. Read slowly. Let the energy move through you as you move through it.

After each section or transmission, pause for a moment. Close your eyes. Breathe deeply. Let whatever arises come and go without judgment. You're not here to analyze these words or believe in them. You're here to feel them. Let them awaken what's already within you.

Read with your heart, not your mind. These transmissions are meant to be absorbed through presence, not thought. The truth in these pages isn't meant to be agreed with or debated. It's meant to be remembered.

Take breaks when you need to. Sit with what resonates. Let the energy integrate before you move on. There's no rush. The journey of remembrance unfolds in perfect timing.

Read this book like a meditation. Feel it more than you think it. The awareness you're looking for isn't hidden in the words, it's in the silence between them.

PART I

THE REMEMBERING

This first part is where the seed of awakening begins to stir within you. It's where remembering replaces searching and the illusion of separation starts to fade. What follows isn't a lesson but a mirror, a reflection of your own Consciousness calling you home. These pages carry the living frequency of remembrance, revealing how vibration shapes your experience of reality and how awareness transforms everything. Each passage is a doorway back into what you already are, beyond belief, beyond effort, beyond time. As you move through these words, let them move through you and reveal what has always been awake beneath the noise of becoming.

∞

FROM DARKNESS TO LIGHT

I was born in 1986, and for most of my life I was asleep to who and what I truly am. I grew up like most kids did. I thought I was normal and like every other kid. I rebelled a lot growing up. I always did whatever I wanted and refused to conform to social and societal norms. Starting at a young age, I learned that having money made life much more comfortable and convenient than not having money. I promised myself at a young age that I'd never allow myself to be poor and do whatever it took to ensure I had financial freedom. Money and materialistic possessions became my motivational driving force.

My life of crime began when I was only twelve years old, back in 1998, when I was in the sixth grade. This was back before the internet had taken off to what it is today. I acquired hundreds of *Playboy* magazines at no cost and had the brilliant idea to sell them at my school. It was a perfect hustle and very lucrative. Hormones were running wild in the pubescent boys I went to school with. The demand for my product was high, and I had zero competition. I could set the price to whatever I wanted. At twelve years old, I walked around with several hundred dollars in my pocket at any time. As I got older, the market demand changed, and so did my product. I started selling marijuana to other teenagers that I knew from the area. This was my full-time job. I eventually turned into a street pharmacist and sold whatever I could get my hands on in large quantities. I was making excellent money and thought I had life all figured out. I was constantly getting the newest toys, nicest electronics, and jewelry. I always had an attractive girlfriend on my arm decked out in diamonds. I thought that this was what life was all about. I felt this was what I was supposed to do with my life.

Naturally, selling the drugs turned into doing the drugs in large amounts. After my father died in 2013, I went very deep into addiction, injecting heroin and cocaine together, commonly known as speedballing. After he passed, I completely withdrew from the world. For a decade, I rarely left my bedroom. The only time I left my bedroom was to get drugs or sell drugs. My whole life, I'd felt like something was missing within me. Society had always taught me to look externally to fill the void within me. I always thought if I had the new toy, new phone, or new girlfriend, that I'd feel better, that I'd feel whole. It never worked out that way, though. My addiction and compulsiveness became so bad that I had significant open wounds on my arms due to several infections in my blood at various injection points. My arms looked like Jared Leto's character Harry Goldfarb's arm from the movie *Requiem for a Dream*. I had several black holes that were severely infected. My blood was turning septic, and I was dying. Around this time, I'd set the intention that I was going to quit the drugs cold turkey, and I didn't care if it killed me. I had a lot of fear because I'd quit cold turkey before, and it was the most excruciating and miserable six months of my life. I remember when I quit cold turkey before; I couldn't do anything except lay in the fetal position for months because my stomach and body were in so much pain.

When I set the intention to quit the drugs, it was the strongest intention I'd ever set, with the utmost conviction. Around this time, I came across the audiobook *Autobiography of a Yogi* by Paramahansa Yogananda. I'd never been a religious or spiritual person before, but after listening to some of that audiobook I was very intrigued. That audiobook resonated deeply within me. Some of the things Paramahansa Yogananda talks about I found to be absolutely amazing and miraculous. I was fascinated by the power of Consciousness, and I yearned to know more. Before this, I'd never tried yoga or even considered meditation. However, I set the intention to become a yogi. I set this intention with as much conviction as I'd set the intention to quit the drugs. When I did this, something in me changed. It's hard to describe in words exactly what I was experiencing. It's something that can't be understood by the analytical mind. It must be experienced, and it can never be understood.

I didn't know what was happening within me at the time, but I found out afterward that my *Chakras* were activating. I stayed true to my intentions and chose to stay in a positive state, no matter what manifested. I couldn't understand why I wasn't feeling the debilitating withdrawal symptoms from the drugs I'd previously experienced when I quit cold turkey. Synchronicities started to occur in an extremely overwhelming fashion, so frequently and rapidly that I thought I might be going insane. I had no idea what synchronicities even were at that time. I started hearing voices in my head. One of the voices that I'd hear was my father's voice. I could hear him guiding me, telling me everything I was supposed to do next. The things I was doing made no sense to me. I didn't know why I was doing those things. All I knew was that as long as I kept taking physical action on whatever my father told me to do, the more synchronicities flooded into my experience, and the better I felt. My mother, stepfather, sister, and all my friends thought I was experiencing psychosis. They all said I needed to go to the hospital to have my open and infected wounds that were turning septic treated with antibiotics, to have a psych evaluation, and to be put on medication. I wholeheartedly refused any and all medical attention. I didn't care if I lived or died. Every fiber of my being told me not to seek medical attention, fully accept whatever manifests while staying in a positive state, surrender completely to the Universe, and let it unfold precisely how it's supposed to.

Throughout this time, I had no real idea what was happening within me. All I knew was that choosing to act on whatever my intuition told me to do, no matter how scary, uncomfortable, or life-threatening it might be, only made me feel better and better. I realized after the fact that by doing so, I was transcending my fear and ego and dissolving every belief system within myself. As a result of doing this, more of my *Chakras* continued to activate, and in the process, made me feel better than I'd ever felt before, better than any drug had ever made me feel. I kept following my bliss, riding this wave wherever it led me, exuding nothing but gratitude for what I was experiencing.

I didn't care if it was psychosis. I remember saying to my friend, "if this is psychosis, then everyone should be insane because this feels absolutely amazing, way better than what I believed was normal or possible."

The reason I was feeling so good was because I kept raising my frequency by transcending fear and ego and choosing to stay in a positive state no matter what manifested. I was quite literally healing my physical body, and by taking action, I was aligning my *Chakras* and tuning my entire being into my Soul's core vibrational frequency. I continued to follow my bliss in every given moment. Then, a few days later, after I'd fully accepted that I was going to die, I sat down, and without even trying to meditate, my eyes closed on their own. I fell into a very deep meditative state known as *Samadhi*. When I was in that long, deep *Samadhi* state, my *Pranamaya Kosha* (energy body) was so vibrant that I literally healed my physical body. When your *Pranamaya Kosha* is vibrant, your physical body must follow suit. After opening my eyes from *Samadhi*, I've never been the same. I now experience everyone and everything as myself, in full unity. The illusion of separation, *Maya*, has disappeared. By fully accepting death, I transcended the last fear I had that was anchoring me to the physical and material world, my physical body and life. Doing so allowed my final *Chakra*, the *Sahasrara* (Crown *Chakra*), to become active and opened me up to Universal Consciousness, in which I remembered everything. I remembered why I chose this incarnation. I remembered other lifetimes, and I remembered that I'd started something in another life that I chose to continue in this one.

Also, I remembered why I chose to be a drug addict in this incarnation. I chose to be a drug addict because I needed to experience the spectrum of frequency from one polarity to the other, from the polarity of fear, negative, and low frequency to the polarity of love, positive, and high frequency, the highest frequency of authenticity, my ultimate frequency. By experiencing polarity, I was given the wisdom needed for this life's path. I've always been a strong skeptic. However, I've continuously remained open-minded throughout my life. Our society and our scientists try to tell us what to believe. They say something is impossible simply because they haven't been able to prove that it's possible yet. I've never bought into that belief. I've always believed anything is possible and that it must be proven impossible before I'd even consider believing that to be true.

Through the circumstances I chose to manifest in the form of being a drug addict, having my open and infected wounds turn septic and begin to kill me, were the ultimate catalyst for transformation to happen within me. I needed to know experientially, without a doubt, that what was happening within me wasn't psychosis or hallucinations. Neither myself nor anyone else can deny that the healing of my physical body without the aid of any medical attention or even the use of soap isn't only possible but a proven fact. It was very important that I was able to open the minds of my friends and family once they were able to see with their physical eyes what was happening right in front of them. Once someone sees something with their own two eyes, the only reason they wouldn't believe it to be true is if they're closed-minded. The frequency that you're attuned to within yourself determines what you can perceive in physical reality. If they can't perceive it, it's because of a fear frequency resonating within themselves, not allowing them to open their minds to other possibilities because it challenges deep-seated negative and limiting beliefs within themselves that they aren't willing to address yet.

Furthermore, I needed to have something in my experience to compare against this feeling of blissfulness that I'd experienced by raising my frequency and falling into *Samadhi*. I'd been on the brink of drug-induced psychosis before from my drugging days. I needed to know that what I was experiencing was something very different and extremely profound so that I wouldn't allow the fear that my family and friends were projecting onto me about refusing medical attention to resonate within me. If I'd allowed their fear that they were projecting onto me to resonate within me, even for a moment, it would've lowered my frequency. It would've prevented my *Sahasrara* from fully activating, and the energy wouldn't have completed its ascent. I never would've fallen into that state of *Samadhi*, and I would've died.

After that *Samadhi* state, I set the single intention that I wanted everyone on the planet to be able to experience this. I gave away my worldly possessions and all my money to people living on the street. Physical and material things no longer interest me. I wasn't expecting to still be alive, and I wasn't sure what to do next. I remembered why I chose this incarnation, to share my experience and help others raise their own frequency. As a result, it helps the planet and the collective Consciousness benefits greatly. Now I wander around the world hitchhiking with my backpack. I help people I meet along the way to raise their frequency. They usually invite me into their home, and I stay with them for a couple of weeks to a few months, or however long it takes to guide them as they heal, dissolve their limiting belief systems, transcend fear and ego, and experience total transformation. At this stage of my journey, everything I have is from gifts or contributions, and I'm supported through people's generosity and synchronicity. I've never felt better in my entire life, better than I ever could've imagined. Once you touch your *Anandamaya Kosha* (bliss body), only then are you truly free.

This was the moment my old life dissolved completely. What began as darkness transformed into light, revealing that everything I'd ever feared was only pointing me back to myself. The experience of *Samadhi* showed me that physical reality itself is a living reflection of the frequency we're choosing to reverberate at. What follows is how that realization unfolded into direct knowing, the mechanics of vibration and the way Consciousness manifests in physical reality.

THE NATURE OF PHYSICAL REALITY

The most important thing anyone can do for themselves and others is to raise their frequency. The yogic sciences are a technology designed for inner transformation by raising your frequency. Yoga means union. It's one of the greatest tools for well-being. Through yoga, you can dissolve every belief system within yourself, transcend fear (ego), and unite your individual Consciousness with Universal Consciousness. However, there's also another way you can choose to raise your frequency. The highest frequency is authenticity, then gratitude, and then love, in that order. Our Higher Self communicates with the physical self through the sensations in our body, known as bliss, passion, or excitement. The physical self responds to the Higher Self through the actions we choose to take. If you're willing to act on your highest passion, your bliss, to the best of your ability in every given moment, with no need to force any particular outcome, and no assumptions or expectations about how it unfolds or what the outcome will be, while choosing to stay in a positive and pleasant state no matter what manifests, examining your beliefs and letting go of fear, negative, and limiting beliefs that are no longer relevant for you,

you'll manifest the life that's in total alignment with your Higher Self. In raising your frequency continuously by becoming more of your true self and walking your authentic path, you'll become your Soul's core vibrational frequency. Therefore, as a result, you're raising your vibration to your highest frequency of authenticity.

When you act on your passion, you're communicating to your Higher Self that you're listening to your own guidance and willing to allow the highest form of your intelligence to take the wheel and steer your physical life. By staying in a positive and pleasant state no matter what manifests, the physical self demonstrates to the Higher Self that it has learned its lesson and is now ready for the next one. You're showing your Higher Self that you're now capable of the next lesson and the next circumstance to be manifested by your Higher Self that aligns with your highest passion and, in the form of unconditional support, provides you everything you need to continue acting on your passion. Things will start to happen in your life through synchronicity that may look like magic, and others won't be able to believe how it's possible. The Universe has your back. It's always supporting you. Nowhere is it written that the Universe expects us to suffer. That's a fear-based, negative, limiting belief some of us have chosen to believe. It's the opposite. The Universe is always supporting us unconditionally. We are beings, which means we choose how we want to be. If someone chooses to vibrate at a fear-based, negative, low frequency, then the Universe says, okay, this is what you're choosing to vibrate at; here's more of that energy. If someone chooses to vibrate at an authentic, grateful, love-based, positive frequency, then the Universe says, okay, this is what you're choosing to vibrate at; here's more of that energy.

The reason why my experience happened so quickly is because I was literally on death's doorstep. I was dying, and I didn't have any time to waste. I maintained the awareness at the forefront of my Consciousness that I wasn't promised tomorrow, or even the very next moment for that matter. So, in every given moment, whatever my Higher Self communicated to me in the form of my bliss or passion, I acted on it immediately without hesitation. I wasn't sure why I was doing the things I was doing. However, I intuitively knew that taking action immediately would be in my best interest. It didn't matter what I was doing or who I was with. The moment my Higher Self presented something else for me to act on, I did just that. I remember several times I'd be in the middle of a conversation with a friend and, without even saying goodbye or explaining myself, I'd get up, put on my shoes, and walk out the door. I knew they wouldn't understand what was happening within me, and I didn't expect them to, nor did I care. I didn't even know what was happening within me. I could feel that something very profound was happening within me, but I wasn't sure what it was. I just knew I had to keep riding the wave to see what this was all about. I realized through my experience afterward why I was doing the things I was doing.

My passion became yoga and helping others raise their frequency. I became passionate about being passionate. I acted on my highest passion, and what excites me most is assisting others to raise their frequency. I understand that all Consciousness is connected and that the most important thing I can do to help others raise their frequency is to raise my own. This is exactly what I did and continue to do without letting my analytical mind get in the way or allowing any fear to resonate within me. I simply continuously acted on all the things my Higher Self presented in front of me in every given moment. Not caring one bit what the circumstances were, I fully accepted whatever manifested. I chose to stay in a positive state by continuously radiating gratitude for this experience we call life. I did this intuitively in every single moment, one hundred percent of the time. I didn't care if I lived or died. It made no difference to me. All I knew was I was feeling better than any drug ever made me feel, better than I ever could've imagined was possible. I fully accepted that whatever happens is what's supposed to happen. I was willing to ride this wave of bliss, and if that meant death, then so be it. I chose to continue acting on the unknown because I'd rather die figuring out what this blissfulness was than go back to my old life that was familiar and comfortable.

Every fiber of my being told me to refuse medical attention. I experienced everything neutrally, formed no opinions, and stayed completely immersed in the present moment, the ever-expanding now, one hundred percent of the time, to the point where I didn't even think of what the negative consequences of refusing medical attention could be. I literally stayed in a positive state no matter what manifested, expressing nothing but gratitude for this profound experience I'd been blessed with. I continued to do this until I became in full alignment with my Higher Self, with my Soul's core vibration. Then one day I sat down, and without even trying, my eyes closed on their own, and I fell into a very deep meditative state known as *Samadhi* that lasted for about five hours.

As my *Kundalini* (dormant spiritual energy) rose and became fully awakened, it ascended through each *Chakra* until it reached my *Sahasrara*, where I dissolved into the stillness of *Samadhi*.

I was vibrating at such a high frequency, with so much energy rushing through me, that I literally healed myself. After opening my eyes from that *Samadhi* state, I've never been the same. Every cell in my body was bursting with blissfulness. To give you an idea, the closest thing I can compare it to is being on an extremely high dose of ecstasy and psilocybin mushrooms at the same time, but without being impaired or inebriated. In fact, it's the opposite. I'm super alert and hyper-aware. Comparing it to ecstasy and psilocybin mushrooms doesn't even come close to describing what this truly feels like. It can't be replicated with a chemical. When you dissolve every limiting belief system within yourself, when you transcend all fear and ego, and your Consciousness unites with Universal Consciousness, there's no possible better feeling. It's pure bliss.

Since that *Samadhi* experience, it's as if the veil that we incarnate with has disappeared entirely. I remembered everything. I remembered why I chose this incarnation. I remembered, from a Soul level, why my Higher Self chose to manifest every single circumstance that I experienced in my physical life. I've been able to perceive how the very structure of physical reality is built. I've realized experientially that separation is an illusion. My state of being now is such that I'm in a permanent state of *Samadhi*, and I experience everyone and everything as myself. I've realized through my experience that there's only one energy, one Consciousness, and it's expressing itself in infinite manifestations. I'm neither the body nor the mind. I am the one energy. I am the one Consciousness. I am pure awareness. I am All That Is, and so are you. All is One.

If you act on whatever it is that you're passionate about and excites you the most and take it until you can't take it any further, then the next thing that presents itself to you in the form of your highest excitement or passion, act on that to the best of your ability, taking that as far as you possibly can in the same way, thus repeating the process in every given moment. You'll continuously raise your frequency, therefore enabling this experience that we call life to be a never-ending expression of your passion, your true self, your highest frequency, and manifesting in the process a life of total and complete fulfillment.

Success isn't about achieving a goal or having things go the way you expected them to. It's about being okay with yourself in every given moment, even when things don't go the way you thought they would. Even when you're not okay, that's okay.

The purpose of life isn't to arrive anywhere or to accomplish anything. There's nowhere to go. The process itself is the point. You're not here to reach a final destination. You're here to discover more of who you already are. As long as you're doing your best, that's enough. That's true success.

THE FORMULA TO RAISE YOUR FREQUENCY

Apply this in every given moment to the best of your ability.

1. Follow your bliss. Act on your highest passion, whatever excites you the most in every given moment to the best of your ability taking it as far as you can until you can't take it any further, with no need to force any particular outcome, and no assumptions or expectations about how it unfolds or what the outcome will be.
2. Choose to stay in a positive and pleasant state no matter what manifests. What that means is to choose to attach a positive definition to every circumstance. It's not about what happens, it's about what you do with it. If you use every circumstance in a positive way, by defining it in a positive way that serves you and aligns with what you prefer, that's how you continuously stay in a positive state. Find the silver lining in everything.

3. Continuously examine your beliefs and identify fear/negative/limiting-based beliefs that are no longer relevant for you. Dissolve those beliefs by letting go of them and no longer identifying with them. What you believe to be true is what creates the manifestation process. What are you choosing to believe to be true?

DAILY MANTRA

A mantra is an effortless and powerful way to reprogram your subconscious. Say this out loud to yourself daily.

Circumstances don't matter, only my state of being matters. It's not about what happens. It's about what I do with it. Circumstances don't matter, only my state of being matters. It's not about what happens. It's about what I do with it.

The more you repeat this to yourself, the more you will effectively reprogram your subconscious to operate in a positive way. If you find yourself starting to feel fear frequency in the form of stress, depression, anxiety, or any unpleasantness, and you would like to transmute that fear frequency into love frequency, do the following.

1. Say out loud to yourself with conviction,
   "Circumstances don't matter, only my state of being matters. It's not about what happens. It's about what I do with it. Circumstances don't matter, only my state of being matters. It's not about what happens. It's about what I do with it."

2. Choose to be in a positive/pleasant state of being by attaching a positive definition to every circumstance, no matter what manifests.
3. Start behaving that way mentally, emotionally, and physically toward your circumstances.

YOGA/MEDITATION

Meditation can be a powerful addition to daily life. However, if you prefer not to meditate, that's okay. The principles I'm sharing can still work for you. What's meant to unfold within you will unfold regardless. It isn't necessary, but it often deepens what's already unfolding within you.

I use a simple guided meditation called *Isha Kriya* to introduce meditation to the people I work with, because it opened a profound doorway into stillness and awareness for me when I first began. It's a free 12-minute practice available online.

What I did was I started practicing *Isha Kriya* first thing in the morning at 4:30 a.m. That's a significant time in the morning to practice your *Sadhana* (spiritual practice), which offers maximum benefits. I found a nice private lake with a secluded area down by the water where I would go every morning to practice *Isha Kriya*. I would bring my journal three-ring binder with me. I'd sit down directly on the ground, allowing the frequency of the planet to reverberate through me while meditating.

I practiced *Isha Kriya* for a couple of days, and then on the next day, I went into my first *Samadhi* state. At the end of *Isha*

Kriya, at the part where it says to slowly, very slowly open your eyes, I thought only five or ten seconds had gone by after that. However, when I opened my eyes, I noticed the sun had moved its position significantly in the morning sky. When I looked at my watch, I noticed an hour and a half had passed. I had no idea what had just happened. All I knew was I felt this wave of bliss that I couldn't describe or understand happening within me, and I didn't want to lose that feeling.

I started journaling my experience. Around this time, while journaling, my hand started writing on its own. Information I had no previous knowledge of was being written by my hand and my pen. I had no idea where this information was coming from. I wrote repeatedly, "Follow your bliss with no fear. Follow your bliss with no fear. Follow your bliss with no fear." That's precisely what I did. I found out later that what was happening through me was a form of channeling called automatic writing. I did exactly what my journal told me to do. I continued to follow my bliss, my highest excitement, in every given moment.

The following morning, after practicing *Isha Kriya*, the same thing happened. I fell into another deep state of *Samadhi* which lasted for two and a half hours. I felt an even more significant and profound wave of bliss bursting within me that I couldn't describe or understand and didn't want to lose, so I continued to follow my bliss in every given moment with no fear. I acted on all the things my Higher Self presented to me, through synchronicity in the form of my bliss and highest excitement, while choosing to remain in a positive and pleasant state no matter what manifested.

Then, after a couple of days or so, I had raised my frequency to such a high bandwidth in a very short span of time that I sat down, and without even trying to meditate, I fell into the longest, most profound state of *Samadhi* yet, which lasted four and a half to five hours.

I maintain my highest frequency of authenticity by continuously following my bliss and choosing to stay in a positive and pleasant state no matter what manifests.

Kriya Yoga has been a powerful foundation for me, and it's how I start each morning. My morning practice usually lasts about two to three hours and includes *Asanas*, *Pranayama* breathwork, and deep meditation. *Kriya Yoga* is a powerful technology that supports physical, mental, emotional, and energetic well-being. By practicing *Kriya Yoga*, it is possible to balance your *Prana* (life force energy) in such a way where people have cured themselves from several different autoimmune diseases. I personally met one individual who had shared with me that she cured herself of two autoimmune diseases by practicing *Kriya Yoga*. She was a teacher I trained with.

FEAR FREQUENCY VS. LOVE FREQUENCY

Fears we continuously manifest circumstances to learn to transcend:

- Fear of inadequacy
- Fear of being uncomfortable
- Fear of what others choose to think and feel
- Fear of not being in control of our circumstances
- Fear of lacking/losing
- Fear of being alone

Once you choose to let go of the fear/negative/limiting beliefs within yourself, and no longer allow fear frequency to resonate within you, because of you manifesting circumstances to learn to transcend the fears listed above, then you are truly free.

Fear Means:

- Boundaries
- Walls
- Exclusion/exclusiveness
- Discrimination
- Expectations
- It's limited/limiting
- Resistance to what is (insisting it be different)
- *No*

Love Means:

- Unconditional support
- Zero discrimination
- Zero expectations
- Boundless
- Limitless
- No walls
- Complete acceptance of all that is
- *All-inclusive*

Check in with yourself throughout the day. "Ask yourself." "Are my actions and/or thoughts exhibiting fear or love?" We continuously manifest circumstances that give us opportunities to make the choice to transcend fear and to transform ourselves from fear frequency to love frequency. If you choose to keep this awareness at the forefront of your consciousness, you will be more conscious and aware of what frequency you're choosing to vibrate at, thus allowing yourself to maintain the perception and awareness needed during challenging circumstances to make a different choice if that's what you prefer.

THE JOURNAL PROCESS

Step 1:

Journal all of your raw feelings, thoughts, and emotions in as much detail as possible. Whatever you're feeling is okay. There's nothing wrong with what you're feeling. Own your feelings.

For example:

I feel insecure about the scars on my arms. I never leave my house unless I'm wearing a long-sleeved shirt because I'm worried about what other people will choose to think and feel about my scars. I fear what other people will say about me. I feel a lot of guilt and shame because I've wasted so much of my life abusing my body and injecting speedballs. In society, the worst type of drug addict, the bottom of the barrel, has always been viewed as the heroin junkie. Being a drug dealer, I was always high and around people who were always buying drugs from me, and yet I still felt ashamed to let any of them know that I was injecting speedballs. Even though we were all using drugs, heroin always carried a very negative, shameful, dirty connotation. I couldn't let anyone know.

Step 2:

Go back through it with fresh, unbiased eyes and objectively apply the fear frequency versus love frequency page to it. Identify your fears and write them down.

Every emotion you ever feel, positive or negative, you feel because you believe you have to. Understand that all feelings, positive and negative, stem from a belief system within you. If you're feeling a fear-based negative emotion and you're unsure why, it's because you're doing it unconsciously.

For example:

I have the fear of inadequacy resonating within me very strongly, the fear of what others choose to think and feel, the fear of not being able to control my circumstance, and the fear of being uncomfortable. During this time, I didn't let anybody know about my drug use because I also had the fear of lacking or losing and didn't want to lose those relationships with those people, and I also had the fear of being alone.

Step 3:

Ask yourself, "What must I be choosing to believe to be true that would make me believe I have to feel the way I do about myself or my circumstance?" Write it down.

Everything is a projection and a reflection. All of existence is neutral. The energy that you put into it is the reflection you see back. No person's thoughts, actions, circumstances, or situations can influence you or make you feel anything. It's only once you choose to believe whatever fear or negative belief someone projects onto you to be true that you then believe you have to feel that way, proving that you're doing this to yourself and that you're choosing to feel this way.

It doesn't even have to be a direct projection from another person. You can overhear something on TV, in a conversation, or in passing, and if you choose to believe it to be true, it becomes active in your field. If that belief causes a negative emotion, it's because it's a low-frequency fear-based belief creating distortion in your frequency. It's simply a vibration you've taken on that doesn't belong to you.

For example:

I chose to believe that being a drug addict is bad and that having track marks means I'm a loser and a waste of life. I've wasted so much of my life chasing drugs and throwing money away on them. Even though I was a drug dealer, all the people in my physical world, all my customers and everyone I knew, labeled heroin as the worst drug you could possibly do. They all believed that heroin junkies were below them, that they were better than heroin junkies. In the media, on TV shows, on the news, and throughout society, heroin addicts are always portrayed as the lost causes of the world, the worst of the worst, the bottom of the barrel.

Step 4:

Now that you understand that you can choose to not believe that limiting negative fear-based belief, choose to redefine it in a positive way that serves you the way you prefer.

Realize that you choose how you experience your life. You manifest all of it to learn how to transcend fear and transform yourself into authenticity, love, and positive frequency. All pain is a result of resistance to the natural self, the authentic self. Whatever it is you're manifesting, understand that you're manifesting it because it's relevant for you. If it wasn't relevant for your experience, you wouldn't manifest it. I no longer have any fear-based negative thoughts or emotions because it's no longer relevant for me to experience those thoughts or emotions. It's because I consciously choose not to allow fear frequency to resonate within me by maintaining my highest frequency of authenticity.

Remember that circumstances don't matter; only your state of being matters. Choosing to stay in a positive and pleasant state by attaching a positive definition to every circumstance that manifests is how you raise your frequency. Your frequency, your state of being, is all that matters. It's not about what happens. It's about what you do with it. It's about how you choose to respond to it. Only your state of being matters. Love means zero discrimination, so you have to be able to not discriminate against anyone or anything for any reason because you, your Higher Self, manifested all of this for the physical self to experience. All Consciousness is connected, and everything is a projection and a reflection.

If you have an issue with someone, your issue isn't with them; it's something within yourself you haven't been willing to address yet. If someone has an issue with you, their issue isn't with you; it's something within themselves they haven't been willing to address yet.

For example:

I choose to no longer believe that about myself. I no longer see the scars on my body as something shameful. I no longer care what anyone chooses to think or feel about me. I choose to no longer feel that my life as a drug addict was bad or that it was a waste of my life. I choose to use my scars as a positive display, almost like a badge of honor, showing others that if I can do it, so can they.

Step 5:

Now identify the lesson behind the circumstance. What's the lesson? What did you learn? What were you willing to learn?

Write out why you're grateful for that circumstance because it was needed for your Consciousness, your Soul, to learn, grow, and expand. Write that you're grateful you manifested the circumstance and that you chose it because you were willing to grow and not run from it. Take full responsibility for all of it.

When you can recognize that every challenge, every pain, and every fear has served you in a positive way, you begin to see the perfection in everything that's ever happened in your life. Gratitude becomes the bridge between what was and what is. Through gratitude, you unify with your Higher Self and integrate the lesson into the present moment.

You begin to realize that the people who triggered you were never the enemy; they were the reflections you needed to see what was still unhealed within you. Their behavior only brought to the surface the limiting beliefs you hadn't yet transcended. When you perceive this clearly, judgment and discrimination dissolve, and compassion arises.

When you find a way to say thank you for every moment, when you find a way to be grateful for every single circumstance, what you're actually doing is closing the loop. You're completing the process. You're completing the thought. This is absolutely vital to practice in every moment, with every experience, because gratitude allows you to fully receive the lesson and then let it go. When the loop is closed, the mind no longer needs to keep returning to it. The thought is complete. This is how gratitude helps prevent compulsive thinking, where the mind loops endlessly between memory and imagination. Gratitude completes the experience, integrates the lesson, and frees you to remain present.

For example:

I choose to feel grateful for my scars because I understand that everything in my life happens exactly the way it's supposed to happen so that I can grow and become the person I am today. I'm grateful for all of my friends projecting their fear onto me in the form of discrimination, from their beliefs that junkies were the bottom of the barrel and the lowest of the low, because by doing that, they showed me what beliefs I needed to dissolve within myself. I'm grateful for the lessons they taught me and the opportunities they provided for me to look within and dissolve the negative beliefs that aren't in alignment with who I truly am. The person I am today can use what once caused me pain to inspire others in a positive way that brings me more fulfillment and joy than any drug ever did.

Step 6:

Positive affirmations are how you cement this entire process into your subconscious mind.

The first five steps rewire your subconscious by bringing unconscious fear-based beliefs to the surface, redefining them consciously, and integrating the lesson through gratitude. Step 6 is what reinforces those new beliefs and gives your subconscious permission to fully accept them as the new narrative.

This step is important because your subconscious learns through repetition. The more you consciously write to yourself in this way, the more you reprogram your subconscious to reflect who you're choosing to be now, instead of who you were conditioned to believe you were in the past.

Instead of compulsive thoughts looping through your mind saying, "I'm not good enough, I can't do this, I messed up, why did I do that, what's wrong with me," you begin to replace that internal dialogue with a new one that's rooted in awareness, self-trust, and self-love.

For example:

I am perfect exactly as I am.

I can't make a mistake because I'm willing to learn from everything, and when I'm willing to learn, mistakes don't exist.

I'm a powerful being without limitations.

I love myself.

I believe in myself.

I deserve everything I desire, and everything I desire is already coming to me.

All I have to do is choose to remain in a positive, pleasant state and enjoy the ride.

I choose to enjoy this beautiful human experience that I'm so blessed to be living.

Thank you, Universe, for all of your love, support, and guidance.

I'm doing great.

I've never felt better in my entire life, far beyond anything I thought was possible.

Keep going.

Keep your foot on the gas.

Keep building momentum.

Keep becoming the process, because the process is the point, nothing else matters.

These are just examples of positive affirmations you can choose to write for yourself. You don't have to use these exact words. Anything you choose to write, as long as it's written in a positive way and feels authentic to you, will work beautifully. Write what feels true for you. Write what supports you. Write what reinforces the beliefs you've consciously chosen. Allow yourself to be creative with this and keep expanding on it.

When practiced consistently, these affirmations don't feel forced. They feel natural. They become familiar. Eventually, they become automatic. This is how your subconscious adopts the new identity you've consciously chosen and sustains it without effort.

Integration:

Once you've completed this process, take a moment to recognize what you've just done. This is how you reconnect with your Higher Self through awareness.

Journaling is one of the most powerful tools you'll ever use. When you give yourself fully to this process, your Higher Self may begin communicating through you, sometimes even in the form of automatic writing, as it did for me. I encourage you to stay consistent and attentive, to record everything that comes through, and to keep journaling as often as you can.

One of the keys to this transformative process is the journaling itself. If you find it challenging to start writing, that's okay. All you have to do is put pen to paper. Start writing anything, anything at all. Begin by writing out five to ten things you're grateful for. Once you start writing, more will come through you. The more you practice this, the more your subconscious will naturally flow onto the page.

Your journal becomes your living manual. It becomes the most important book you'll ever own because it's literally you having a conversation with your Higher Self.

In my experience, my journal is the most important tool I have. I wasn't expecting to live through what I've lived through. After I physically healed myself in *Samadhi*, I didn't know what to do next. My Higher Self channeled through me in the form of automatic writing, providing everything I needed to know. Everything that my hand writes into my journal, I act on. This is how I've continued to navigate my life entirely through intuition.

Journaling is also how you dig deep into your subconscious and bring unconscious fears to the surface. It's how you identify and address your fears, transcend them, and become grateful for experiencing them because they were needed for your Consciousness to learn, grow, and expand. This process can be used to heal emotional trauma and to rewire your subconscious mind so you stop forming new fear-based limiting beliefs and continue expanding into higher levels of awareness and unity with Source.

Even if a situation happened long ago, if it still carries

emotional charge, it's alive within your Consciousness. When you write from awareness, you dissolve distorted beliefs that no longer serve you and integrate new beliefs that align with your true self. Writing becomes the alchemy that transforms what was into wisdom, freeing you to create consciously rather than react unconsciously.

CLOSING REFLECTION

By choosing to follow your bliss and act on your highest excitement in every given moment to the best of your ability, while maintaining a positive and pleasant state by attaching a positive definition to every circumstance no matter what manifests, and by continuously letting go of fear-based beliefs that are no longer relevant for you, you will raise your frequency and align with your Higher Self. You raise your vibration to your highest frequency, your Soul's core vibration of authenticity.

Remember, success isn't about achieving a goal or having things go the way you expected them to. It's about being okay with yourself in every given moment, even when things don't go the way you want. Even when you're not okay, that's okay. The purpose of life isn't to accomplish something. There's nothing to be done. The process itself is the point. You're not here to reach a final destination. You're here to discover more of who you already are. As long as you're doing your best, that's enough. That's true success.

It's important that you maintain zero expectations because expectations always lead to suffering. Be kind and patient with yourself. Remember, one of the keys to transformation is journaling because it's the tool that allows you to dig deep within your unconscious and subconscious mind to become aware of the fear-based limiting beliefs you're choosing to believe to be true. Refer to The Journal Process pages for guidance.

Just because something happened for me the way it did doesn't mean it'll happen exactly the same way for you. It doesn't mean you're doing anything wrong if your experience unfolds differently. The circumstances my Higher Self manifests for me are exactly what's relevant for my growth and expansion, and the same is true for you. Whatever you're manifesting is perfectly aligned with what your Consciousness needs to learn, grow, and expand.

We are eternal, masterful beings who've chosen to experience humanity. You're perfect exactly as you are. You're one of the infinite expressions of Source, All That Is. Your being, your Soul, is one of the infinite perspectives through which Source experiences Itself. Without you, existence wouldn't be complete. You're a piece of the puzzle, and without your piece, the big picture, the entire puzzle, wouldn't be complete.

You are All That Is.

All is One.

PART II

LIVING CONSCIOUSLY IN THE EVER-EXPANDING NOW

Part II is where remembrance becomes embodiment and awareness becomes action. It's where you begin living what you already know to be true, choosing your vibration in every given moment. This is the movement from theory into experience, from knowing that you're the creator of your reality to consciously being it. Here you learn how to respond instead of react, to align your state of being with your highest frequency of authenticity regardless of what appears around you. Through real stories, living examples, and direct techniques, you will see how every circumstance is an opportunity to practice conscious choice and master your state of being. When you live this way, you realize that life is always happening through you, and when you become conscious, you stop creating from fear and start creating from love, allowing the life you prefer to unfold through you.

∞

TRANSMISSION 1

THE ILLUSION OF CONTROL

Surrender is the gate through which awareness walks itself home.

Physical reality is a school designed by you, for you, to teach you how to transcend fear and dissolve the limiting, fear-based beliefs that you're choosing to believe to be true in the unconscious mind that you're not even aware of. It's a constant mirror in physical form, reflecting back to you the belief systems that you're believing to be true in the unconscious mind. It's there to show you what you need to work on within yourself and what you need to dissolve so you can experience full unity with Source, with Universal Consciousness, and realize that you're a spiritual being choosing to play this game of Consciousness in physical reality as a human being.

We manifest all circumstances to teach us how to surrender. Circumstances are always changing on the surface, the same lessons, just a different paint job. The circumstance will change, but deeper, beneath the surface levels of the circumstance, the lesson is always the same. The lesson is always the same: master your state of being. You do that by dissolving your belief systems and transcending the illusion of fear. This raises your vibration and brings you into more alignment with your Higher Self, your true essence, your authentic self. Fear isn't real. It's simply a construct in our minds that limits us. It's nothing more than an illusion.

It only takes one moment of absolute willingness and total surrender for this to happen. You don't need years of what most people define as spiritual practice like yoga, prayer, meditation, chanting mantras, or ritualistic activity. Are those things beneficial? Yes, they can be, especially if you believe them to be, because whatever you believe to be true is what gets projected into physical reality, and that's the mirror you see reflected back to you. If you believe that's the only way to experience liberation, then that'll be the only way you allow yourself to experience it.

What it truly comes down to is the willingness to accept what is and choose to be at peace with it. For everything going on in your inner world and your outer world, accept it one hundred percent. Take full responsibility for it and choose to be grateful for it, because your circumstances don't define you. You choose, in every given moment, how you want to be. Your life could be mirroring back to you complete chaos. Everything around you could appear to be burning down, completely out of control, but that's the illusion. Your Higher Self is perfectly in control of everything. It's a perfectly orchestrated symphony of vibration. Nothing happens by accident. Nothing is random.

I realized from my own life experience that the Higher Self manifests circumstances that appear extremely challenging, those rock-bottom moments that seem unbearable at the time. Those moments aren't happening to us; they're happening for us. Our Higher Self intentionally manifests those types of circumstances as catalysts, as opportunities to accelerate, to build momentum, so that when we finally choose to let go and fully surrender, we accelerate faster and slingshot further into the light. It's kind of like pulling a slingshot back with a rock in it. The further and deeper you pull into darkness, the resistance we hold toward our circumstances, the greater the potential energy that builds within. If we choose to surrender and let go, the rock releases and flings in the opposite direction, further and faster, the stronger our resistance had been.

My life has been full of these catalyst moments. I'm sure many of you reading this can relate. We've all gone through rock-bottom moments or extremely challenging circumstances that make us ask, "Why is this happening to me? What did I do to deserve this?" I can tell you, dear reader, it's not a negative thing. It's not a bad thing when these circumstances occur. It's actually the greatest blessing because through the Higher Self manifesting those circumstances for the physical self, it's building up the tension of energy within, which creates the momentum that releases once someone chooses to fully let go. It's you pulling your slingshot back further so that in the right moment, when you finally choose to surrender completely, you effortlessly launch into the light. Your *Kundalini* can rise extremely fast, and you can experience spontaneous *Kundalini* awakening and *Samadhi* states just like I did.

One example from my life where I had to learn how to transcend the same six fears all over again came through circumstances that looked and felt extremely traumatic and negative at the time. The story goes like this. When I was nineteen, I had been arrested for drug charges. I moved into a house and didn't even live there for twenty-four hours. The people already living there were selling drugs out of it and conducting their business sloppily. Little did I know, the police were already observing the house, and I was literally moving right into a trap. Less than twenty-four hours after moving in, the house was raided by the task force team. They arrested me along with everyone else living there.

One of the people in that house had a lot of fear from the

arrest, and I completely understood. I did too. I was nineteen, and here I was thinking I might go to prison for who knows how long. It seemed like this person was going to crack under the pressure and inform on the supplier. At that time, I had never met the supplier before, but something inside told me that I needed to take the fall for all of it. My mom's boss, bless his heart, lent me the money I needed to hire the best lawyer in town. I hired him, and he found inconsistencies in how the police handled evidence, picking the case apart skillfully. He worked out a deal with the district attorney that allowed me to take responsibility without informing on anyone. In the end, I got a slap on the wrist, one year of probation and a small fine. I was ecstatic because after a year it would all be expunged from my record. I had been expecting prison time.

This man, the connection, we'll call him Freddy, came into my work one day. I had to get a legitimate job while on probation, so my mother got me a job working at a gas station owned by the company she worked for. One day when I was working, Freddy came in and told me, "Man, I can't believe you did that for me. You don't even know me, and yet you were willing to take the fall to protect me. Anything you need, anything at all, it's yours. Just say the word." What happened is that I had shown this complete stranger total loyalty, and by doing that, it opened the door to organized crime for me.

I was in a lot of debt, needing to pay back my mom's boss for the lawyer, so I chose to go right back into selling drugs. Freddy and I became extremely close, best friends, inseparable. He was truly a brother of mine, and I absolutely know for a fact that he's Soul family. We became so close that when I started dating a woman, we'll call her Amy, tension began to rise between Freddy and me. Amy and I did everything together, and I fell absolutely head over heels in love with her. Freddy got jealous that I was spending most of my time with Amy, and he decided to drive a wedge between us.

One day, I was at home with Amy. I jumped in the shower thinking my life was perfect. I was making great money. I had this beautiful woman I loved and a best friend who was also my business partner. Everything I believed that life was supposed to be about, all the boxes were checked. I thought I had life all figured out. Twenty minutes later, when I got out of the shower, my entire life was turned upside down. I found out Amy had been cheating on me with Freddy, and she had taken my burner phone, my prepaid drug phone, and called all my friends, customers, and connections, telling them I was working with the federal government, with the DEA, and to never talk to me again.

Due to all the fear she projected through the calls she made, and since I had brought her everywhere and introduced her to everyone closest to me, they believed what she said. When I got out of the shower, I'd lost everything in one swoop, my girlfriend, my best friend, my business partner, all of my friends, customers, and connections. I had no idea how I was going to make money. My entire business was gone. The rug had been pulled out from under me. It was shocking, traumatic, and painful beyond words. I couldn't believe it. But my Higher Self had manifested all of those circumstances to give me another opportunity to transcend the same six fears. The circumstance itself didn't matter. It was all about the lesson of transcending fear.

Eventually Amy moved out and started seeing Freddy for a while. Somehow, she and I began talking again, I don't even remember how. But of course, I forgave her. I forgave Freddy too. I somehow intuitively knew that what they did wasn't personal. It came from their own fear of inadequacy, their own fear that they weren't willing to face. Somehow, I had always understood this on a deep level, how fear works, but I wasn't able to connect the dots consciously until *Samadhi*. That was one major catalyst moment in my life, one of many that my

Higher Self manifested long before I was ready to fully surrender.

Years later, my Higher Self would mirror this same lesson in an entirely different way during my awakening in the summer of 2023. I was staying at my mother's house for a couple of weeks, trying to figure out what was happening within me, what I was experiencing. Synchronicities started happening so often that they became overwhelming. I realized later that synchronicities are the external road signs, the outer validation, the reflection that your inner world is coming into alignment. The more aligned you are within yourself, the more you see it reflected back through synchronicity in your outer world, because the outer world is always mirroring your inner world.

During that time, I was experiencing an intense flood of psychic downloads, and it was overwhelming. I learned that psychic information, like everything in the Universe, flows along the path of least resistance. So if it can come through a physical medium, another person speaking the very thoughts you're thinking, a song on the radio, a scene on the TV, it'll come that way first before it downloads directly into you. One example of this was when I was meditating in the spare bedroom at my mother's house. In that moment, I was realizing that my mind is an illusion, that thoughts aren't my own and they don't define me. I wasn't creating my thoughts but rather observing them. The more still I became, the fewer thoughts I had. I'd sit for long periods without a single thought forming, and when they did arise, they came as questions.

I remember asking myself what I was supposed to do next, and the next impulse that came to mind was to go get some pineapple out of the fridge. So I did. As I was walking through the living room, the TV that my stepfather was watching suddenly caught my attention. In that exact moment, the character on the show answered every single question that had just formed in my mind, word for word.

When that happened, I thought someone was playing a sick joke on me. I thought, how is this possible? I'm literally having a conversation with myself through the TV right now. But it wasn't a conversation in the ordinary sense. It was me observing a dialogue from a higher level of awareness. Not knowing what to make of it, I grabbed the pineapple and went to my car to go for a drive. As I walked outside, more questions formed in my mind, and the moment I turned the key, the song on the radio began playing the exact lyrics that answered those questions perfectly.

Again, I thought this was some kind of joke. I truly believed I was losing my mind, that I was slipping into psychosis, because this went on constantly for days. It didn't matter where I went or what I did. The TVs were talking to me, the music was talking to me, even complete strangers sitting at the tables next to me in restaurants were literally saying everything that answered the questions in my mind. When I wasn't sure what to do next, I would make food and bring it to the homeless shelter, handing it out to everyone living on the street. I would sit there with my eyes closed and could hear everything, every sound, every movement, every whisper. My awareness was through the roof. I could sit on a bench and hear the wind rustling through the trees, every car driving by, every bird singing in the distance, the crickets chirping and the frogs croaking. I could hear two people to my left having a conversation, three people in front of me speaking about something else, and people behind me talking about something entirely different, and somehow, all of it was relevant to the thoughts in my mind.

When I opened my eyes, I could see their mouths moving, but what I heard were the exact messages I was meant to receive. I was having a psychic conversation with the entire Universe, and it was being transmitted through everything, voices, songs, TVs, conversations, every sound around me. It was constant. It was alive. None of it was random. None of it was by accident. Every whisper was a reflection of my own awareness speaking back to me.

Free will is an illusion. The only free will you truly have is how you choose to experience your life; you choose your vibration, your state of being. When you surrender, what you're doing is getting out of your own way and allowing the highest form of your intelligence to take the wheel and steer your life. You're not limiting yourself to only manifesting what you think you prefer, because sometimes you have to walk through a door that appears to be uncomfortable or even terrifying to reach the other side, which holds exactly what you've been asking for. When you let go and trust that process, everything unfolds much faster. Alignment with your true self happens naturally and without resistance.

The challenge is that it takes most people a long time to reach the breaking point where they can let go completely. It can take an entire lifetime to reach that one moment of total surrender. Many people go through their entire lives and never reach that moment of total willingness to fully surrender. My entire life, just like your entire life, is a spiritual process. Spirituality isn't thirty minutes or an hour a day on a yoga mat in meditation. Spirituality, at its core, is the willingness to break the self-imposed limitations of the body and the mind. When someone has the willingness to dissolve belief systems, break the boundaries of the mind, and transcend the limitations of the body like I did by accepting death, that is spirituality.

When someone has enough willingness to do that, they can break all limitations of the physical body and of the illusionary mind, and they can completely dissolve and experience *Samadhi*, full unity with Universal Consciousness, the realization that you're not the body, you're not the mind. You're the vast ocean of infinite intelligence. You're Source, choosing to have a human experience. You are All That Is.

If you treat every moment in this school that we call physical reality as your *Sadhana*, your spiritual practice, to let go and become more conscious in every given moment, the unfolding of your awakening and the raising of your vibration will be tenfold. Physical reality is the training ground designed to teach you how to raise your vibration by transcending fear and dissolving limiting beliefs. Everything is spiritual. Physical reality itself is spiritual. It's simply a more dense manifestation of Spirit, of Consciousness. Therefore, your entire life process is your spiritual process.

What I learned from my own experience, the life path that my Higher Self chose for my physical self to experience, in the form of being a career criminal, a drug trafficker, my Higher Self chose these circumstances for a specific reason, just like your Higher Self chose yours. Each path is designed to teach surrender. My life, at any given moment, if I had been caught doing what I was doing, I would've faced a twenty-five-to-life sentence. Yet I still chose that path. It was in my highest excitement. I loved what I was doing, and I was good at it. The cat and mouse game with the law excited me. My Higher Self was constantly giving me opportunities to learn how to surrender control, to stay out of my memory and imagination, and to keep my awareness anchored in the present moment.

It didn't matter if I was driving with hundreds of thousands of dollars' worth of narcotics in my trunk or driving completely clean without any contraband. I drove the same way. I kept my awareness in the now. I didn't worry about what might happen in the future. I didn't vibrate at the frequency of fear, and therefore I didn't attract fear-based outcomes. I was vibrating abundance, love, acceptance, and surrender. On the surface, what I was doing might've appeared wrong or illegal. Some people would've judged me as a bad person, but that's only based on their belief systems. Consciousness doesn't discriminate. Circumstances don't matter. Only your frequency matters. This life, this reality, is nothing more than a dream being experienced through you, through Consciousness exploring itself from infinite perspectives. In this lifetime, the perspective that my Higher Self wanted to experience was to dissolve the beliefs of right and wrong, the fear of what others think and feel, the fear of losing control, of lack, of inadequacy, of being uncomfortable, and of being alone.

Your Higher Self manifests your circumstances to teach you to transcend those same fears. The outer paint job changes, but the underlying lesson remains the same. Everything is built by you, for you, to bring you to that one moment of total surrender and absolute willingness to let all your identities die. Your circumstances don't matter. Only your frequency matters.

When I gave up all control, when I accepted death completely and chose to maintain a high vibration filled with authenticity, gratitude, and love, that was when I fell into multiple spontaneous *Samadhi* states and was able to heal myself. I faced death with grace, and through that, death didn't come for me. During the purification process of my *Kundalini* awakening, where the energy rises through the *Chakras* to the *Sahasrara*, it was vital to remain in surrender and not let fear resonate within me. Many people who experience spontaneous *Kundalini* awakenings unconsciously allow fear to take hold during this natural purification. That vibration disrupts the flow of energy upward and can cause them to create more limiting beliefs because it attracts more fear-based circumstances to manifest into their physical reality.

It can lead to depression, disassociation, and psychosis. Several people have ended up in mental hospitals and heavily medicated due to psychotic breaks from the overwhelming amount of fear-based circumstances that are abruptly manifested into physical reality from their unconscious belief systems. This creates extremely challenging circumstances that they're forced to confront and dissolve. Without knowing how to navigate through it, it can appear to be disastrous. When *Kundalini* awakens, it doesn't care about your job, your family, your plans, or your comfort. It's your Higher Self saying to the physical self, "I'm ready. You've learned the lessons you needed. You've surrendered enough for the process to begin. Now it's time to purify, to dissolve the old, to burn away everything false so that only truth remains." But remember, that moment of surrender isn't the end, it's the beginning of the purification process. You must continue to stay out of your own way by remaining in full surrender as the energy purifies you. If resistance returns during this process, it can become turbulent or appear to be disastrous, since the Higher Self will always keep reflecting circumstances mirroring the fears that still need to be transcended.

Fear is never outside of you. What's outside is an illusion, a mirror showing what you're believing to be true in your unconscious mind. My Higher Self designed my life path perfectly, knowing that I'd have to face death to reach the point of surrender. That was my catalyst moment, refusing all medical help, accepting death fully. When I did that, nothing could faze me anymore. My circumstances no longer had power over me. For days, life reflected every remaining fear in my unconscious mind in rapid succession. I didn't resist any of it. I was yes and yes to everything. Whatever manifested, I jumped into it with both feet, knowing that each experience was there to teach me how to master my state of being, how to stay in a positive and pleasant state no matter what appeared in my external world.

One example of this truth is when I began journaling my experience. My hand would start writing on its own, automatic writing. Whatever my hand wrote to me, no matter how ridiculous, unpleasant, or unreasonable it looked, I acted on it immediately without hesitation because I knew this information wasn't my own. I intuitively knew it was channeled directly from my Higher Self flowing through me. My physical self could understand that information only when it was expressed in a way the mind could comprehend, in written words. What was really coming through was a complex frequency transmission that my Higher Self was translating through vibration. Psychic information doesn't always come through in chronological order or in plain-spoken words. It's more of a feeling, a vibration that has to be discerned and translated for the physical mind to understand and make sense of.

When my hand wrote, "Give it all away," that's exactly what I did. I learned through that experience that my Higher Self chose to manifest those circumstances so I could learn to transcend the fear of lacking or losing, and the fear of not being able to control my circumstances. My Higher Self was carefully orchestrating my life, giving me the chance to willingly let go of the old and make space for the new to manifest. I had no idea at that time what the new would look like. I was still attached to my possessions and to money. To break that limitation instantly, my Higher Self told me to give it all away. I chose to act on that with absolute willingness and in total alignment with what my Higher Self told me to do. By doing that and staying in a positive and pleasant state no matter what manifested, I was able to transcend that fear and raise my vibration.

That willingness to face and transcend fear started the manifestation of new circumstances that matched my new vibration. I had to learn how to navigate life without money or possessions and still stay in a positive and pleasant state through all of it. One time I went to the grocery store because in that moment my highest excitement was to buy some fruit and healthy organic food for dinner. I grabbed a cart and started down the produce aisle, grabbing whatever I wanted and throwing it in. I was completely present, fully involved in the ever-expanding now. It wasn't until I came up to the cashier that I realized I didn't have enough money to pay for it. But in that moment I didn't believe that just because I didn't have enough money in my account meant I couldn't have what I wanted. My intuition told me to go to aisle 3, so I happily followed without thinking about how I'd pay or whether I should put anything back.

I greeted the cashier with a big smile, radiating love and compassion. I asked how she was doing, and she said she wasn't doing well. She was unconsciously choosing to suffer because of one of her circumstances. I helped her reframe it so she could see it as something positive instead of negative. In that moment she became grateful for what she was going through because she realized she'd been choosing to suffer, and she made the conscious choice to stop. By transmuting her fear frequency, by maintaining my high vibration, she raised her own to match mine, and in that moment the Universe took care of me. As she rang up my food, the computer suddenly glitched and cut my total bill in half. I had just enough money to pay for everything. I didn't have to put a single thing back. I got everything I wanted without even trying, without having to figure out the how. I just did the now really well, with full involvement and total awareness in the present moment, and the future took care of itself.

When I no longer believed I needed anything for security or survival, and when I no longer desired anything with expectation, the Universe provided everything effortlessly. This is how you dissolve belief systems that keep you bound to the illusion of separation, to the identity of body and mind. All it takes to experience full unity, to be free of judgment, desire, and expectation, is complete surrender. When you do that, you realize the illusion isn't something to escape, but the flow of Consciousness expressing through you. From this space, you can maintain bliss through anything. You realize you're not the doer. You're not even the observer. You're the stillness and the silence that allows all vibration to take form. You're pure awareness, witnessing the observer observing the doer.

CLOSING REFLECTION

When you truly let go, life stops feeling like something you have to survive and starts becoming something you get to experience. Surrender isn't weakness. It's power. It's the moment you stop fighting with what is and realize that life has been guiding you home all along.

Every circumstance you've ever faced was never punishment or reward. It was a lesson, a reflection of what you were ready to see and release. When you stop trying to control the flow, the river carries you effortlessly. That's when life starts to reveal its deeper intelligence.

Surrender isn't the end of your journey. It's the beginning of real freedom. The moment you stop chasing and start trusting, you discover that everything you've ever wanted has been moving toward you the whole time.

TRANSMISSION 2

AWARENESS IN MOTION

To live consciously is to be aware of awareness itself, to know where your attention is moving, and to choose to bring it back again and again into the ever-expanding now.

Awareness moves through three dimensions, or three faculties of your mind: memory, imagination, and the now. When you master awareness, you learn to live fully in the now instead of compulsively in the others.

The only reason anyone ever chooses to suffer is because of their memory and imagination. Memory and imagination aren't real. They're just thoughts, constructs of the mind. Yet something that happened a moment ago or five years ago in the past gets relived again and again, and people choose to suffer from it in the now. Something that might happen tomorrow, next week, or a year from now causes the same suffering, because they project fear into the future.

The only moment we truly have is right now, the ever-expanding now. What most people define as trauma isn't real, it's an illusion. Emotional trauma, as I see it, is someone choosing to remember something in a negative way that serves them in a way they don't prefer. That's fear in the past, fear vibration, fear frequency stored in memory, and the narrative they tell themselves about it becomes their identity. They replay the same story in their mind and keep choosing to suffer from it.

Fear projected into the future shows up as anxiety, the what ifs, the hypotheticals. When you project fear vibration into the present moment, because your awareness is lost in imagination, you're altering your vibration in the now. Whatever you're vibrating at now starts the manifestation process in physical reality, attracting circumstances that match that vibration.

When we stay stuck in memory or imagination and identify those stories as negative, we frame our experience through fear and victim consciousness. That affects our current vibration and keeps us repeating the same patterns. Have you ever wondered why something keeps repeating in your life? It's because you're stuck on a vibrational level somewhere in your memory that you choose to keep reliving in the same way. You expect the future to play out like the past, so you project that frequency into the present, and that's why you attract similar circumstances. The surface details change, but the deeper lesson is always the same. It's the same lesson with a different paint job.

The more conscious you become in every moment, by mastering awareness and keeping it from drifting into memory or imagination, the more you live in the ever-expanding now, the less you suffer. When you're fully present, there's no room for suffering, because you're only experiencing, only doing. You're fully engaged, fully responsive to everything happening inside and outside of you. When you're fully aware and consciously responding, you stop making a mess of your life by being compulsively triggered. You respond consciously in every moment to manifest outcomes you prefer.

Sometimes the most powerful response is silence. Silence is the ultimate power. Awareness is like light. When it shines into memory, you relive the past. When it shines into imagination, you anticipate the future. But when you keep it here in the now, the light of Consciousness reveals the truth that all existence is happening now, eternally unfolding in this infinite present moment, the ever-expanding now.

To become more conscious in every moment means to make your *Sadhana* not only a part of your daily life but present in every single moment. Bring awareness into every action. Every moment of your life is your spiritual practice. If you treat it as such, if you make every moment your *Sadhana*, you'll overcome compulsiveness like magic. You'll raise your energy, raise your vibration, and learn to look inward into the unconscious mind to discover the limiting beliefs you've been choosing to believe to be true and dissolve them.

You'll learn to consciously respond to fear-based circumstances as they manifest, to transcend them by staying in a positive and pleasant state no matter what appears. By doing this, you continually raise your vibration and expand. The parameters of your experience expand, and you feel less separation from Source, less division within yourself. You begin to experience unity with Source, because you are Source and always connected to it. The illusion of separation comes from fear-based beliefs in the unconscious mind and from compulsive thought patterns and reactivity that lower your vibration and manifest circumstances you don't prefer.

When you make your *Sadhana* every moment, every breath, every movement becomes conscious. You can brush your teeth consciously, walk consciously, eat consciously. Eating especially is powerful when done with awareness. Speaking is also important to do consciously, along with breathing. I'd say for most people the two most difficult compulsions they deal with within the body are eating and speech. When people speak compulsively, that's how they make a mess of their circumstances with others. The more you speak, the more you're programming your mind on a subconscious level to believe whatever it is you're saying.

When you have limiting beliefs and you say things like "I can't do this, I won't do that, I don't want to, I shouldn't, I wouldn't, I couldn't," you're reinforcing it into your subconscious mind that you aren't capable of doing those things. If you're saying it, you're literally programming yourself with your speech. That's what your subconscious mind believes, and whatever you believe to be true deep in the subconscious and unconscious mind is the mirror you'll see reflected back in physical reality. You can never actually do something until you believe it's possible. You'll never make it manifest until you begin to believe that it's possible first.

Breathing is the most fundamental thing your body needs, what life itself needs to continue. Every breath should be taken consciously, with full awareness and full gratitude for every inhalation. When you bring yourself back to the present moment, let's say you're in a challenging circumstance, your awareness wandering from memory to imagination, compulsively looping, just take a moment or two, close your eyes if you must, and take a deep breath through your nose. With that inhalation, put out gratitude for the breath. Put all your awareness, energy, and focus on that single inhalation. Realize that your psychological drama doesn't define you. Your circumstances don't define you. Life doesn't care about your circumstances or your psychological drama. Life wants to continue, and the only thing it needs to continue is your next breath.

Put out gratitude for every inhalation, because without it, you wouldn't be alive. Without it, you wouldn't experience this beautiful miracle we call the human experience. You came to this planet to have a human experience, so choose to enjoy it, that's the whole point. Your circumstances mean nothing. Your thoughts mean nothing. It's only once you choose to believe whatever story you tell yourself about your circumstances, and identify it as negative, that you choose to suffer. Maintain neutrality through all of it. Form no opinions about anything while exuding gratitude for your experience. That's the whole point, to enjoy the ride, because it's going to unfold exactly the way your Higher Mind has already orchestrated it to. Your job as the physical self is to enjoy the ride, to find the silver lining in everything, in every moment. You can only do that when you become more conscious and aware, when you keep your awareness in the present moment, in the ever-expanding now.

Sadhana isn't what you do. *Sadhana* is how you do it, with full awareness, full presence, and full surrender. When every moment becomes a conscious act, life itself becomes your yoga. The key to mastering your state of being, the key to mastering your body, mind, emotion, and energy so that you can be a conscious creator of your reality instead of an unconscious reactor to it, is to respond to everything consciously, not to react. Reactivity is unconscious. Responsiveness is conscious. When you live consciously, you respond from awareness, not from fear. You become the master of your attention, no longer ruled by the mind's compulsive movements. The more you master your state of being by dissolving belief systems that make you believe you have to suffer, or that you must have an issue with anyone or anything, the more consciously you'll live, and the easier it becomes to respond consciously to every circumstance that manifests in your life. You choose how you want to be in every given moment. So why would anyone ever choose to be anything less than blissed out within themselves all day long? You wouldn't do it consciously. If you're experiencing negative thoughts and emotions that you don't prefer, it's because you're doing it unconsciously.

You're reacting to your circumstances based on belief systems in your unconscious mind. Every emotion you ever feel, positive or negative, you feel because you believe you have to. They all stem from belief systems within you. When you learn how to keep your awareness in the present moment, you can perceive on a deeper level why your Higher Self is manifesting certain circumstances for the physical self to experience. From that level of awareness, you can consciously respond to them while maintaining your vibration in a high frequency of authenticity, gratitude, and love. You can transmute fear frequency immediately, whether it's being broadcast from within you or projected at you by others, and change the vibration of your circumstances when you master your state of being.

One truth that speaks to this is when my sister called me a few months ago with some news she had defined as fearful and negative. She works remotely from home in marketing for a large company. She lives in a small town where jobs are limited. She's always been grateful to work remotely from home and make a good living. One evening she called me while I was on the road and said "Tyson don't tell Mom but I just got notified that I'm being laid off. They gave me thirty-days." I told her, "Congratulations. That's super exciting. I'm so happy for you." Of course that wasn't the response she expected. She even said that, then laughed and told me that knowing me, that's exactly what she should've expected.

I told her that it was okay. Stay in the moment now. Don't get stuck in your memory or imagination. Don't get caught in the fear of lacking or losing, or the fear of survival and security around money. All of that will take care of itself if you simply master the present moment. Keep your awareness in the now and keep your vibration high, authentic, grateful, and loving. I told her this was the Universe testing her, aligning her vibration to a higher level so that a new opportunity could manifest, one that matches her frequency. She wasn't losing anything. She was gaining everything. I also told her that one door must close before another can open. The Universe was testing her willingness to stay committed, to learn from her circumstance, because every circumstance is your school to master your state of being. She manifested this experience to learn the same six fears we all face again and again. Every circumstance we manifest is a reflection designed to help us transcend those same fears.

In this particular circumstance she identified the fears she needed to transcend were the fear of inadequacy, the fear of being uncomfortable, the fear of what others choose to think and feel, the fear of not being able to control her circumstance, the fear of lacking or losing, and possibly the fear of being alone as well. A lot of times it's all six. The deeper you go, it's all six. On the surface level you might only be able to identify one or two, but they're all interconnected. I told her that's what it is. It's very simple. You manifested this circumstance. The circumstance itself doesn't matter. The only thing that matters is your state of being, your frequency. You manifested this to learn to transcend these same fears. Respond consciously, knowing this, and do just that.

That's exactly what she did. After she received her layoff notification, she still had thirty days to continue working. When her boss had to deliver her the formal news, her boss was crying because it wasn't her decision and it wasn't easy for her. She still had her job, but she had the responsibility of laying off half of her team, and my sister was one of them. My sister was the one comforting her. AJ told her it was going to be okay and asked if there was anything she could do to support her in that moment. That was the state AJ chose to stay in, grounded, calm, present, grateful.

During that thirty-day period she started meeting one-on-one with some of the leaders she worked under. She didn't go into any of those meetings from a place of fear or victim consciousness. She didn't say "I don't know what I'm going to do" or "How am I going to pay my bills?" She showered them with gratitude. She told them how much she'd learned both personally and professionally over the last seven years. She told them how grateful she was for their guidance, their support, the experience she'd been given, and how much she appreciated everything. She kept her awareness on gratitude, the second highest frequency, and that's how she sustained her vibration through all of it.

From that state of being, by maintaining a high frequency, her name naturally started circulating upward through the company. On the surface it appeared like there were many variables and it appeared like things were happening randomly. On a deeper level that's all just the illusion of physical reality. On a deeper level her Higher Self manifested every one of those circumstances, the layoff, the uncertainty, the appearance of competition and challenge, all of it, to give her the catalyst she needed to transcend fear and master her state of being.

By maintaining a high vibration of authenticity, gratitude, and presence through the entire process she became more aligned and more in coherence with her Higher Self, her true self. The more she stayed in alignment with that high frequency, the more her circumstances reflected that alignment back to her, because our outer world is always a reflection of our inner world. She became in coherence with the vibration of the circumstance she truly preferred. She became the resonance of it. As a result of that alignment she manifested the outcome that matched her vibration. Instead of being laid off and unemployed, she was offered a new job within the company that she actually preferred, doing work she's passionate about and manifested a huge raise in the process. She didn't have to go looking for it. She didn't have to search for anything. It came knocking at her door. She had expected to be laid off and instead was offered a promotion. All she had to do was be willing to close one door and walk through another. In those moments between one door closing and another opening she stayed in a positive and pleasant state no matter what manifested, and that's all she had to do. Physical reality is continuously reshaping itself to match our state of being.

She called me after this happened and told me that she had her aha moment. The aha moment is what I call it when those I've shared this with have spent some time with me, absorbed what they can, and now it's time for them to start applying it. It's those moments where they've tried to understand the things I tell them with the analytical mind, but I always tell them that they can never understand how this works with the analytical mind. It's something that must be experienced. But if they have the willingness to keep their mind open and apply the process of raising their vibration, dissolving their limiting fear-based beliefs, and becoming more conscious in every given moment, they'll start seeing their circumstances mirrored back to them as a reflection of the higher vibration they're choosing to reverberate within themselves. They'll start manifesting what appears to be magic into their life, and they won't be able to explain how it's possible.

Aha moments like that are some of the most beautiful moments to experience, because they're the result of direct realization. I love getting those phone calls from the people I work with when they have these aha moments because it's confirmation to me that they're applying it, that they're choosing to become more conscious. They're focused on their ultimate well-being. They've realized that their circumstances don't matter, only their state of being matters. If they keep their focus and intention on becoming more conscious in every given moment by raising their vibration, their circumstances, like magic, will take care of themselves. They don't have to figure anything out. They simply learn how to be in the ever-expanding now, with full awareness.

When she called me, she told me she'd had her aha moment. She said she finally realized everything I'd been telling her. She told me it had now become part of her awareness, part of her experience. She was overflowing with gratitude, for me, for her circumstance, for herself. So much appreciation. Her cup was overflowing, and she said she'd never felt better in her life. She was witnessing first hand the magic of the Universe when you become a conscious creator, not a compulsive reactor.

This is the power of being fully present in the now, in the ever-expanding now. This is the power of conscious response versus unconscious reaction. The more conscious you become, the more you literally become a conscious creator of your reality. You can create it how you prefer based on the vibration you're choosing to reverberate at within yourself instead of unconsciously reacting to compulsive thought patterns that you're believing to be true, which create circumstances you don't prefer, circumstances you identify as negative or traumatic. The more belief systems you dissolve, you begin to realize there's no such thing as positive or negative. Everything's actually neutral. Whatever belief system you're choosing to believe to be true about it in your unconscious mind becomes the mirror, the reflection that you see back in physical reality. You choose how you experience your life. You choose your state of being, your vibration, your frequency. If you choose to find the silver lining in every given moment, that's how you stay in a positive and pleasant state no matter what manifests.

Whatever compulsive thoughts or feelings you're having in any moment, there's nothing wrong with them. However you're choosing to think or feel in any given moment is okay. It doesn't matter if the thoughts you're having you identify as negative or if the emotion feels negative, that's okay. Staying in a positive and pleasant state means attaching a positive definition to your circumstances, finding the silver lining in everything, so you can use it in a way that serves your growth and expansion instead of keeping you stuck and contracted in victim consciousness. It's like how two people can experience the same event, and for one it just rolls off their back, while the other chooses to suffer from it and be traumatized by it for years. Both experienced the same thing, but each chose to experience it differently. One person didn't believe they had to suffer, so they didn't suffer at all because they didn't hold an unconscious belief making them believe that they had to. The other person had belief systems in their unconscious mind that made them believe they had to suffer, and made them believe they were a victim of it. They weren't even aware they were choosing to do this. So they continued to suffer unconsciously until they realized they were doing it to themselves, until they chose to redefine their so-called traumatic circumstances from the past in a positive way that serves them in the way they prefer. It's about fully accepting everything for what it is, without forming opinions about it, while simply choosing to enjoy the ride by exuding gratitude for your experience and fully surrendering to the process and the natural flow of the highest form of your intelligence.

CLOSING REFLECTION

The ever-expanding now is the doorway to eternity. When you rest your awareness here, the illusion of time dissolves and you realize you've never left home. If you do the now really well, by maintaining absolute awareness and total involvement in the present moment, the future takes care of itself. The now is all there is. The now is where freedom and liberation lie. Liberate yourself and choose to master your awareness and keep it focused in the ever-expanding now.

TRANSMISSION 3

THE TECHNIQUE OF CONSCIOUS CHOICE

This transmission explores how conscious choice transforms your entire experience of life. When awareness guides your actions, you move beyond compulsion and step into true freedom.

After healing the infected sores on my arms, the scars left behind from the injection points of speedballs, a mixture of heroin and cocaine, my Higher Self manifested another perfect circumstance to teach me how to heal myself through awareness. One day, while riding my bicycle, I lost balance doing a wheelie and crashed hard, tearing the skin off my left knee. At that time, I was already living on only pineapple, eating just a few bites a day and no longer drinking water. I had already begun using this simple technique, pushing myself to dissolve every limitation of my body and my mind. I was consciously choosing to break through the conditioning of what doctors, scientists, and society say is possible. I wanted to see for myself what the body and mind are truly capable of when guided by Spirit. The energy flowing through me was so powerful that after the crash, I didn't even feel it. I didn't even realize the skin had torn off my knee until I looked down and saw my leg gushing blood.

This technique can be applied to anything, everything. What I did is I waited two minutes before every single bite, before I did anything. Every time I wanted a bite, I would hold a little square of pineapple, about one inch by one inch, in my fingers, and I would stare at it for two minutes with full awareness, full energy, and focus on this present moment. I would ask myself, "Do I want it? Do I need it?" I continuously asked myself this for two minutes, doing nothing else except this practice. After the two minutes, if I told myself, "Yeah, I know I don't need it, but I want it," then I would take it, and I would fully enjoy that bite. I would enjoy it even more than I'd ever enjoyed another bite before because I took it consciously. I savored every flavor, all the juices pouring into my mouth, the natural sugars, the rehydration sensation because I wasn't drinking water, and before I'd eat another bite, I'd wait two minutes and ask myself the same thing. I would do this technique again and again. Do I want it? Do I need it? I did this so much that I got down to only five bites a day.

I remember one specific time I was really pushing myself, breaking the limitations of my body and my mind. I was with a friend of mine, and we went to go help one of his friends dig a bobcat out of the ditch. It was one hundred plus degrees Fahrenheit that summer day, and the sun was very hot. Four of us guys were trying to dig this bobcat out of the ditch. My buddy's wife came running out with huge glasses of ice water for all of us. Everyone chugged down their water. They were struggling due to the high heat and the demanding physical activity. I chose to pour the water on my head to cool me down. I refused to drink it. I continued working, helping to dig this bobcat out of the ditch.

After a couple of hours of doing this, when we went back to the truck, I pulled my little cooler out that had my pineapple in it, and I did this technique. I looked at it for two minutes while I held it in my hand, and I said, "Do I want it? Do I need it?" I thought to myself, well, I think I need it. I've been programmed by society to believe I need it. Due to everything I unconsciously chose to believe to be true in the past, I definitely believed I needed it. Did I want it? I think I want it. I think I'm thirsty. But I told myself in that moment, if I don't have this one bite of pineapple right here, right now, it won't kill me. So therefore, right here, right now, I don't need it, and I don't want it, and I put it back.

I continued to do this for about a month, living on only five bites of pineapple a day. My weight didn't fluctuate. My energy actually was higher than it's ever been in my life. My perception was heightened beyond measure. My awareness was off the charts. The things I could start perceiving were mind-blowing. The amount of energy I had was extremely intense all the time, because I wasn't wasting any energy digesting food. I wasn't putting many impurities in my body. Even healthy food holds impurities that the body must digest and purify, which takes enormous energy. Since I was barely consuming any food, and the food I was consuming was the most positive *Pranic* food I could've chosen to eat, which is fruit, my subconscious bodily actions within the digestive system were extremely minimal. The less subconscious actions that are being performed in any given moment, the better. I was realizing that I could sustain myself from my *Prana*, life-force energy.

I've also shared this technique with the people I work with. It's helped several of them quit smoking, drinking, taking illegal narcotics, relying on pharmaceutical pills like antidepressants, Adderall, Xanax, and more. It's helped them to become more conscious and start eating healthier foods. It works with compulsive speech and compulsive thought patterns. This simple technique is so powerful. The more you integrate it, before you do anything, everything, you realize how much of what you've been doing was unconscious and compulsive. You move from unconscious compulsiveness to conscious response.

Another simple technique that I recommend everyone to use is to begin each morning by writing out three intentions.

1. I choose to become more conscious in every given moment.
2. I choose to stay in a positive, pleasant state no matter what manifests.
3. I'm willing to do whatever is needed in the moment.

Below these three intentions, write the reminder:

My circumstances don't matter. Only my state of being matters. It's not about what happens. It's about what I do with it.

This is a very simple technique, but when practiced daily it reprograms the subconscious. It tells the subconscious that this is what matters most. By writing these intentions, you're establishing your priorities at the level of vibration.

These three intentions are the only things that truly matter. They must be your top priority in every given moment. Your circumstances don't matter, because if you take care of these three intentions, your circumstances will take care of themselves. When you become conscious enough to respond to everything rather than react, you're consciously creating. You're doing the now really well.

After writing your intentions, you can also write out whatever you believe you need to do that day. There are no wrong answers. Write in the order of what excites you the most and then go about your day. Use your day as your *Sadhana*. Use every moment as an opportunity to become more conscious, to stay in a positive and pleasant state no matter what manifests, and to be willing to do whatever is needed in the moment.

When you practice this, you begin to see that every circumstance is your mirror. Every challenge becomes your invitation to awaken deeper. When you begin your day from this place of conscious intention, you move through life as a deliberate creator rather than a victim of circumstance.

The more you write these three intentions, the faster you'll accelerate your transformation. When you live this way, awareness becomes automatic. Every desire, every action becomes another opportunity to choose consciously.

Let's say you're trying to quit smoking. You do this technique, you wait two minutes and you say, do I want it, do I need it? After two minutes if you say, I know I don't need it, but I want it, that's okay. Enjoy that cigarette. You could also apply it in between every drag of the cigarette and as a result you'd be smoking less than normal because the cigarette will continue to burn while you wait the two minutes in between each drag. The key is to absolutely make sure you enjoy the cigarette. Stay in a positive, pleasant state while you enjoy it. Don't beat yourself up for smoking, because you're not trying to quit smoking. What you're doing is becoming more conscious in every given moment. If you have the willingness to do that, the quitting of smoking will become effortless. You'll quit the smoking as a consequence of becoming more conscious.

One day you'll wake up and you'll look at that cigarette and you'll say, I no longer want it and I no longer need it. You'll put it down and you'll never crave it again because you put it down consciously. You didn't force yourself to try to quit something. You didn't buy into a belief system that you needed to quit something or that someone else is trying to make you quit. No. You did it as long as you wanted to, and you enjoyed every single moment while indulging yourself in that cigarette or whatever compulsion you have. The more you raise your energy and your awareness, one day you'll just wake up and say, I no longer want it and I no longer need it. You'll put it down and never pick it up again because you put it down consciously. That is the power of conscious choice, the first step toward true liberation.

When you begin to live consciously, awareness becomes your way of being rather than something you practice only during meditation. You start to see that every moment invites you to stay awake, present, and aware of what you're choosing to give your energy to. Conscious choice becomes effortless when your awareness expands beyond thought and merges with direct perception. One of the most powerful ways I learned to cultivate this kind of awareness in everyday life came through a simple practice that I began doing intuitively during my own transformation. It's a meditation with the eyes open, a way of merging awareness and action so that focus and presence become one.

Some people might call it a walking meditation, but it can be done anywhere. Here's how the practice works. Pick a point in front of you, any point at all. It could be a mark on the wall, a tree, a candle flame, anything. Fix your gaze on it and hold that focus as steadily as you can. Blink as little as possible, just enough to keep your eyes comfortable. Pour all your awareness into that single point. At the same time, breathe consciously. Observe each inhalation and each exhalation. While maintaining your focus on that one point, let your peripheral vision open. You can see everything happening around you. People moving, cars passing, light shifting, sounds echoing in the distance. You're aware of everything, yet you don't move your focus from the point in front of you.

What this does is it trains your awareness to expand while staying centered. It balances the mind between concentration and openness. It strengthens your intuitive perception, the part of the brain connected to creative flow, the right hemisphere, and the hippocampal region responsible for spatial awareness and memory. You can think of it as exercising the muscle of presence. I used to practice this technique all day. It didn't matter where I was, sitting on a couch, walking, or even driving my car. When I was driving, I'd stare at the license plate of the car in front of me. That way, if the driver hit the brakes, I could respond instantly without losing my focus. My awareness stayed anchored on the license plate, yet I could still see everything else. Cars passing on the opposite side of the road, bicyclists on my right hand side, birds flying above, trees blowing in the wind. I maintained full focus on the plate while being completely aware of everything around me, and through it all, I was breathing consciously. Slow, rhythmic breathing. Breathing as I describe in another transmission.

I don't suggest anyone practice this while driving, just to be safe. I'm simply being transparent about how I chose to practice it. Practice at your own risk. The meditation itself is extremely beneficial, but it's wise to begin when you aren't operating a vehicle or machinery. Start in stillness. Start seated. Let your breath become your only movement.

This open eyes meditation helps merge the inner and outer worlds. It allows you to remain deeply present in movement, in action, in life. You're not escaping the world. You're uniting with it. The gaze becomes your anchor, the breath your rhythm, and the awareness your bridge between form and formlessness. This is meditation in motion. It's how you train the mind to stay awake while living fully in the now. As you continue this practice, remember that every gaze, every breath, every moment of focus is an opportunity to become more conscious.

Another time I started practicing this technique was when I was driving across the country doing a big drug run. I didn't know it at the time, but I was intuitively doing what I now call the Open Eye Meditation. I would set the cruise control and drive for long extended hours on the freeway without stopping.

I'd pick a point in front of me, usually the license plate of the car ahead, and I'd just stare at it. I'd stay totally focused on that single point without really trying to do anything else. I wasn't thinking about my breath or consciously observing it. I wasn't doing any of this on purpose. It was just happening. As I drove, I could see everything through my peripherals, the cars passing on the other side of the road, the trees blowing in the wind, the birds flying overhead. I wasn't in my memory or imagination. I was completely present. I was in this deep, trance-like focus, and over time, something strange started to happen.

I began falling into very deep states of meditation, so deep that my eyes would start trying to close on their own. One time, this happened and I swerved off the road and almost hit a semi. At that time I had no idea what was happening, but after the fact, through this experience, I realized how powerful this practice is and why people shouldn't do it while driving. It's not safe. The state it brings on can be extremely deep, and if you're not prepared or properly grounded, your awareness can shift out of the ordinary waking focus needed for physical tasks like driving.

When I was doing this for hours on the freeway, my legs started bouncing up and down on their own, shaking violently like I was dancing. I wasn't making them do it. I couldn't stop it. My whole body started vibrating and shaking, especially through my stomach, my *Manipura* (solar plexus *Chakra*), my hips, my *Muladhara* (root *Chakra*), and up into my chest into my *Anahata* (heart *Chakra*). I didn't understand what was happening. I just knew it was intense and uncontrollable. I was on a tight schedule, so I couldn't pull over and stop. I had to keep going.

While I was driving, I was experiencing waves of bliss. It felt like I was high on drugs, but it had been hours since my last injection of a speedball. Typically with heroin, you need to do a shot every four to eight hours before you start going into physical withdrawal. Your body begins cramping, your stomach twists, you get the sweats, nausea, and shakes. Sometimes you start puking or having diarrhea. It's a miserable experience, and I knew it well. I was used to driving fourteen hours straight, and by the time I got to my hotel, it had usually been fourteen hours since my last injection. I'd always feel terrible by then. The first thing I'd do was shoot up so my body could feel at ease, so I could sleep and get up early to keep driving. When this started happening, everything changed. After one of those long drives, when I got to the hotel, I felt super high, better than any drug had ever made me feel. I wasn't feeling any withdrawal symptoms. Naturally, I was confused. I couldn't explain what was happening. Me being as stubborn as I was, I never thought to consult a doctor or research what was happening inside me. I just let it flow. Whatever was happening, I leaned into it. I accepted it. Once again, it was my Higher Self teaching me to fully surrender.

While driving, to prevent my eyes from closing on their own, I turned the music up as loud as it would go and started headbanging violently to the rhythm. I was fully immersed in the music, completely absorbed in it, giving my entire being to the sound. There was no thought, no past, no future, just the ever-expanding now. I did this for hours, shaking and moving and staying totally present. At the time, I thought I was just trying to keep myself from falling asleep, but later I realized what was actually happening. My body wasn't trying to fall asleep. My *Kundalini* was becoming active and wanting to ascend.

This had been trying to happen naturally at different points in my life, but I kept getting in my own way through the drug use, the fear, the resistance. What I was experiencing on that drive was my Consciousness trying to fully open, trying to merge with the infinite, and my body was responding to the energy moving through it the only way it could. The violent shaking, the uncontrollable movement, the full body vibration, it was all energy, all Consciousness expanding through me. At the time I didn't know what was happening, but later I realized it was one of the first times deep meditation was trying to happen spontaneously through me. You don't need a temple or a cave. You just need presence. I don't recommend anyone do it while driving. That was part of my experience, part of my awakening, but for your own safety, practice it only when you're still, where you can surrender completely. The power of this meditation is real, and if you give yourself to it with enough intensity, it can take you very deep, very fast.

Looking back, I can see that what happened on that drive was the first time I truly felt what *Kundalini* energy was like. It had been trying to rise through me many times before, but my addictions, the impurities I was putting into my body, and the resistance I still carried kept pulling it back down. Each time it would rise, I'd unconsciously get in my own way through fear, doubt, or lack of surrender. But those moments were never failures; they were lessons. They were my Higher Self teaching me how to let go more deeply, how to trust the current moving through me. It wasn't until I set the intention to quit the drugs, aligning my thoughts, emotions, and actions with that single intention, that the energy was finally able to move freely. Without realizing it, I was dissolving belief systems, mastering my state of being, and bringing myself into complete alignment. That intention marked the beginning of the final ascent. The energy began to rise stronger than ever before, burning away everything false, and when I fully accepted death and surrendered completely, my *Sahasrara* opened.

Months later, after my awakening, I was so out of balance because my central nervous system went through a massive upgrade. My entire body was buzzing with energy that was flowing through me at such a rapid rate that I could barely handle it. It felt like my whole system was being rewired from the inside out, like new pathways of energy were forming faster than I could integrate them. During meditation my body would start shaking and trembling on its own. My spine would become perfectly erect, as if an unseen force were gently pulling me upward by the crown of my head. It felt like someone was stretching me from within, lengthening my spine and aligning every vertebra. Even though the movements looked intense, they didn't hurt. I could feel the energy flowing upward through me, surging along the spine toward my *Sahasrara*, and it was beautiful.

One day while I was driving, I saw a family of ducks walking across the road. The mother and father duck led the way and behind them followed a line of tiny ducklings. The moment I saw them, my full attention went to the way they were moving their heads. Their necks were gently bobbing up and down in the most subtle way, almost imperceptible. It reminded me of that time months earlier when I was driving cross country, violently shaking my head to music while *Prana* surged through me, trying to find balance. As I watched the ducks, I intuitively knew the Universe was showing me something. At that exact moment, the lead duck stopped in the middle of the road and looked right at me, making direct eye contact. I felt the confirmation immediately. This was no coincidence. I realized the ducks were there to teach me how to balance my energy through gentleness instead of force.

From that day forward, whenever I listened to music, I began to nod my head very subtly to the beat. Music has always been a huge part of my experience. It's one of the most powerful tools I've found to anchor myself in the ever-expanding now. I'd be fully immersed in the rhythm, the melody, the vibration of it, and I'd gently nod my head, barely moving, in perfect harmony with the sound. It was as if the frequency of the music was harmonizing the *Prana* within me, guiding it to flow through my entire energetic system, from the

Muladhara through every *Chakra* all the way to and through my *Sahasrara.*

It was like my Higher Self had intuitively taught me how to balance my energy through music. What used to be violent, uncontrolled movement had transformed into grace and rhythm. Through gentleness, everything began to harmonize. I could feel the energy moving through me calmly and evenly, no longer surging out of balance. I practiced this for days, breathing consciously, feeling the energy stabilize, feeling my entire being become lighter and more balanced. Most of the time when I was listening to music, I was fully immersed in it, letting the beat and rhythm guide my subtle movement. It was as if the sound itself was helping me align my frequency. Sometimes when I'd sit in total stillness, completely thoughtless, I'd have a thought arise and my head would gently nod yes on its own. I wasn't doing it intentionally, it just happened. I came to realize it was a biofeedback mechanism between me and my Higher Self. The gentle nods were a form of communication, confirming when something was in alignment with truth.

The ducks had shown me the way. The violent movement became grace, chaos became rhythm, imbalance became balance. Through gentleness, the energy became harmonized and balanced.

CLOSING REFLECTION

Conscious choice is the bridge between who you think you are and who you truly are. It's how the unconscious becomes illuminated, how compulsion becomes awareness, and how awareness becomes liberation.

Every thought, word, and movement is an invitation to awaken. Each moment asks only this: will you respond consciously or react compulsively? When awareness chooses itself, life stops feeling random. You begin to see that every circumstance is perfectly mirroring the Consciousness that is choosing to experience it.

To live consciously is to live as freedom itself. You no longer chase change, you become the change. You no longer wait for peace, you are peace. You no longer try to control life, you allow life to express itself effortlessly through you.

When you choose to be conscious in every given moment, you discover the miracle was never in the circumstance, but in the awareness of it. The now becomes your temple. Every choice becomes your *Sadhana*. Every breath becomes your liberation.

TRANSMISSION 4

BREATH OF AWARENESS

Your breath is the bridge between your body and your Spirit. It is the rhythm of creation flowing through you in every moment. To become aware of your breath is to awaken to the ever-expanding now, where Consciousness breathes itself through you.

Your breath is the most fundamental aspect of your life. If you have the willingness to learn how to master your breath, you will master your Consciousness. You'll master your body, mind, emotion, and energy. One of the simplest techniques anyone can use in any given moment to become more conscious is breathing consciously. That means to be fully aware and observing every inhalation and every exhalation, not breathing in any particular way, simply observing every inhalation and every exhalation. When you do this, you're anchoring yourself into the present moment. You're placing your awareness on a bodily function, and this keeps your awareness from drifting back into memory or imagination.

If you bring intention into your breathing, for example with every inhalation simply thank the Universe for this next breath, realizing that without it you wouldn't be alive, you can immediately release the psychological dramas playing out in your mind. You can dissolve the pull of memory and imagination when you anchor your awareness in the present moment through your breath. The breath is the perfect bodily function to focus your awareness upon because it connects the physical and the subtle.

When you intentionally put out gratitude for every inhalation, the breath works differently within you. Gratitude is the second highest frequency, and the more you practice gratitude in every given moment, the easier it becomes to sustain your vibration in that frequency indefinitely. Conscious breathing is a vital, simple, and yet profoundly powerful way to anchor your awareness in the present moment while truly feeling grateful to be alive. Feel every inhalation, the sensations in your nose, the air traveling down your chest and into your lungs. Feel the oxygen flowing throughout your entire body.

The deeper your awareness becomes as you raise your vibration and become more conscious, you can begin to perceive the subtle body. You can start to perceive *Prana*, the life force energy that flows through you. You begin to feel not just the air entering and leaving your nose, but the energy that sustains your existence and gives life to your physical form. This whole process is essentially a complete rewiring of your subconscious mind. It's a total deletion or formatting of your hard drive and the installation of a new operating system, one that runs smoothly and free of corruption, one that reflects your conscious choice. When you breathe consciously, you begin to live consciously.

If you find yourself in an extremely challenging circumstance and you choose to stay in a positive, pleasant state while maintaining awareness and control of your breath, you rewire your subconscious. When you breathe slow, steady, and calm, your subconscious mind believes you're safe and secure because the body naturally breathes that way when it feels safe and secure. If you remain calm and aware in a challenging circumstance, you stop producing the stress chemicals that arise from unconscious fear, like cortisol. You stop letting the body run its old programs. When you breathe consciously and consistently, you begin creating new neural pathways in the brain. The brain begins to function as a unified, coherent tool rather than fragmented compartments of thought.

It's absolutely crucial that, whenever possible, you breathe through your nose rather than your mouth. One simple and yet powerful technique that I'm always practicing goes as follows. The exhalation must be longer than the inhalation. When you exhale, make a soft resonant sound from the pit of your throat, with your mouth closed but your throat voice engaged. This is not optional. This is integral.

When you make the exhale longer than the inhale, you signal safety to your body. The vagus nerve becomes more active during the out-breath, and the nervous system begins to regulate instead of react. The heart rhythm slows and steadies. Breath and heartbeat start to synchronize. As the body settles, the mind follows. Thoughts lose urgency. The inner noise softens. Body and mind begin moving into coherence, into repair, into calm.

Modern science can actually measure this shift. It's called Heart Rate Variability, or HRV. HRV doesn't create calm. It shows how adaptable your nervous system is by measuring how your heart rhythm changes in response to breath and internal state. When your breath slows and your exhale lengthens, your heart rhythm becomes more responsive instead of rigid. That responsiveness is resilience. Within HRV there's a component that reflects parasympathetic activity, the calming side of your nervous system. As you practice long, gentle nasal exhalations, that calming influence increases. Your system becomes less reactive and more coherent.

From a yogic perspective, breath is understood differently. In yogic science this is explored through *Swara Yoga*, the study of breath currents moving through the *Ida*, *Pingala*, and *Sushumna Nadis*. Nasal breathing is said to balance these energy channels and harmonize the hemispheric functions of the brain. The scientific model and the yogic model use different language, but both recognize breath as a direct regulator of state.

I once experimented deeply with nostril control. For more than a week I plugged my right nostril with a tissue and breathed only through my left. The calm I entered was profound. My mind softened and I floated in clarity. I wasn't sure whether it was from *Samadhi* or from the breathing itself, but I felt a deep contact with my inner frequency.

Later, I learned that some yogis intentionally plug the right nostril for an entire solar cycle, roughly twelve years, as a disciplined practice. In yogic understanding, the right nostril is associated with *Pingala* and the analytical mind. The left nostril is associated with *Ida* and intuitive awareness. When I restricted the right nostril, my analytical mind quieted and something more receptive opened. The shift was undeniable.

One truth from my experience is that I intuitively began practicing a breathing technique one day and made it my way of being from sunrise to sunset. My intention was unbroken. I rarely missed a conscious breath, and when I did, I immediately brought my awareness back. I'll share my exact technique in a moment, but first know this, breath is the anchor of all embodiment, the foundation of your state, your frequency, your reality.

One day I woke up at 4:30 a.m., the time I would always rise to practice meditation, and I drove to a private lake I had discovered. There was a paved path leading up a hill and around a corner that opened onto a dirt trail. Down that trail was a spot at the edge of the lake where I would sit inside a large hollowed-out tree, perfectly shaped like a seat made for me. That morning I was doing my breathing technique the entire drive. When I arrived, I left my shoes in the car and walked barefoot, continuing the breathing technique without missing a single beat up the hill, around the corner, and onto the dirt path.

As I reached the path, I saw a woman with two large dogs. I must have startled them because the woman panicked. She lost control of the leashes and the dogs broke free, growling and running toward me. In that moment, I didn't flinch. I maintained absolute awareness and discipline with my breath. I crouched down to one knee, extended both arms with a hand toward each dog, and stared directly into their eyes. I remained completely still within myself, in body and mind, not allowing my awareness to wander into the imagination of fear or the hypothetical thoughts of being attacked. I was fully anchored in presence. This was yet another circumstance my Higher Self manifested for me to surrender, to transcend fear, to master my state of being, and to maintain my awareness out of memory and imagination, anchored fully in the now.

The dogs stopped in their tracks, confused. They turned around, whimpered, and ran back to their owner. The woman was in shock. She told me that her dogs were usually vicious and attacked people. She couldn't understand how they had suddenly stopped and retreated. At the time I didn't know either. Later I realized what had happened. By consciously controlling my breath, I was regulating the chemical processes within my body. You've probably heard the saying that dogs can smell fear. That's not exactly true. What dogs actually detect is the hormonal change that occurs when the body experiences fear, the release of cortisol and other stress hormones. Dogs respond to that chemical signal. Since I was breathing consciously, my body wasn't producing any stress chemicals. There was no fear for them to smell. I was radiating gratitude, love, and compassion. I experienced myself as those dogs. There was no separation and therefore no threat. That's why they turned away.

Afterward, I continued down the path, sat in my hollowed-out tree, and began to meditate. That's when I fell into my first spontaneous *Samadhi* state. When I opened my eyes from that *Samadhi* state, I thought only fifteen minutes had passed, but an hour and a half had gone by. At first I thought my watch was broken, but when I looked up, the sun had moved dramatically across the sky. It's difficult to describe what it felt like when I opened my eyes. Experiencing absolute emptiness within yourself, so empty that you can't even experience the emptiness, is beyond words. All I could feel was pure bliss radiating from me in every direction. I was boundless. I was limitless. I began to experience everything and everyone as myself. It felt as if I were suspended in waves of bliss and clarity beyond anything I'd ever known.

The sensation was indescribable, as though every cell of my being were illuminated from within and bursting with ecstasy, yet the ecstasy itself was awareness. I could see through the illusion of separation. It wasn't even about seeing; it was more of feeling through the illusion. The lake was like glass, smooth as ice. In that moment a duck landed on the water, sending ripples outward. As the ripples spread, my heartbeat changed and matched the rhythm of the ripples on the lake. I had no idea what had happened or how I was able to perceive such a subtle change within myself. My awareness was boundless. It elevated into pure clarity. I was able to perceive subconscious brain activity while fully awake, in a coherent waking state. The brain always functions across multiple frequencies at once, but most people can only perceive one at a time. In that moment, I could perceive several.

It was as if the deep stillness of meditation, the dreamlike quality of theta, and the alert clarity of wakefulness were all happening together in perfect harmony within my awareness. When the duck moved and the ripples shifted, my heartbeat adjusted perfectly with them. I had no explanation for it. All I knew in that moment was that reality wasn't what I'd been taught it was. I was experiencing life as a living simulation, an illusion of form sustained by vibration and perception.

The breathing technique that came to me intuitively and that I began using goes as follows. I trained myself to breathe through my nose at all times unless absolutely necessary. Nasal breathing must become your baseline. Even when you're doing physical activity, train yourself to breathe only through your nose as much as possible. It's also vital that we breathe from the diaphragm. If you look at a baby, how a baby breathes, you see their stomach moving. That's because babies naturally and instinctively know how to breathe properly from the diaphragm. Unfortunately, as we grow older, we forget this and begin breathing shallowly into the upper chest instead of breathing deeply from the diaphragm. That's not the proper way to breathe.

The fewer breaths you take per minute, the more you begin to perceive. Subtle sounds become noticeable. Visual details sharpen. Sensory awareness expands beyond what you normally register. Your awareness multiplies and your perception heightens. Your perception is everything. The more you can perceive, the more profound your experience becomes. Again, it all begins with becoming more conscious in every given moment and choosing to breathe consciously.

Before I get into the actual technique, I should mention something that I learned later on through direct experience. When you practice breathing through the diaphragm, it's important to do so on an empty stomach. Don't try this technique unless you've waited at least four hours after your last meal. So here's the technique that intuitively came to me one day, the technique that I began practicing literally in every moment of my life. I would inhale fully by pushing my stomach out. On the fullness of breath, I'd hold for three, five, or ten seconds. Then I'd exhale through my nose by pulling my stomach in, full exhalation, and on emptiness of breath, I'd again hold for three, five, or ten seconds. I'd then repeat this process. Inhale fully through the nose, pushing the stomach out, hold for three, five, or ten seconds, then exhale through the nose by pulling the stomach in, full exhalation, and hold again on emptiness for three, five, or ten seconds. Over time I was able to expand those holds up to sixty seconds, sixty seconds on fullness of breath and sixty seconds on emptiness of breath. I was barely breathing at all. Even when I was doing physical activity, I practiced this breathing technique. When I was riding a bicycle or walking, I'd still breathe this way. When I was riding up a hill, sometimes I couldn't hold for any seconds, but I still breathed through the diaphragm in this same manner. What I was able to start perceiving as a result revealed dimensions of awareness I hadn't known were possible. The subtle moments of pause in between the breaths are where all the magic happens.

CLOSING REFLECTION

The breath is the bridge between the physical and the nonphysical, between body and Spirit, between illusion and truth. The breath is the pulse of the Universe moving through you. It is not something you do; it is something that is being done through you. When you breathe consciously, you begin to experience yourself as the breath of creation itself. You're no longer a separate individual taking a breath; you're the breath breathing you. Every inhalation becomes a return to Source, every exhalation becomes a surrender back into the infinite.

Through this practice, you learn that the breath carries intelligence far beyond the mind. It holds the memory of your Higher Self, the silent knowing that guides every cell, every heartbeat, every moment of your existence. When you listen to your breath with full awareness, you begin to hear the voice of that intelligence whispering through you.

This is the power of conscious breathing. It unites you with the ever-expanding now. It purifies the body, steadies the mind, and opens the gateway to deeper perception, to the silence where the voice of your Higher Self begins to speak. It was from this silence, from this living breath, that the words of my Higher Self began to flow through me, the birth of what I now call automatic writing.

TRANSMISSION 5

FOOD IS FREQUENCY

Food is energy taking physical form, Consciousness becoming substance. When you eat with full awareness, you aren't consuming matter, you're communing with life itself.

Eating can be done consciously or compulsively. If you eat consciously and make it a part of your daily *Sadhana*, it'll function differently within you. If you think of your body as a machine, the fuel you put into it should be what your machine needs and what it runs best on. Taste is simply an incentive to eat, but what you should eat is what your body calls for. There are many dimensions to food. There's the dense dimension, where food provides sustenance to the physical body in the form of calories, vitamins, and minerals. But there are deeper dimensions that connect to your subtle body, your *Pranamaya Kosha*, and directly affect how your *Prana*, your life force energy, flows through you.

In the yogic culture, food is classified into three qualities:

Sattvic, *Rajasic*, and *Tamasic*, often referred to today as positive, neutral, and negative *Pranic* food. The most positive *Pranic* food is fruit because it's mostly water and leaves very little residue or taxation in the body. Think of fruit as jet fuel that burns clean and passes through your system quickly. Vegetables are also positive *Prana*, with some exceptions, being garlic, onion, and eggplant, which are considered *Tamasic* (negative *Prana*). Tomatoes and potatoes are usually labeled *Rajasic* (neutral *Prana*). Sugarcane, coffee, tea, refined white flour, processed grain products, and meat fall under the *Tamasic* (negative *Prana*) category. According to yogic understanding, meat can take seventy-two hours to pass through your system, while fruits and vegetables pass much faster.

Modern science has begun to echo this wisdom. When you eat fruits and vegetables, your gut microbiome, the ecosystem of bacteria within your digestive tract, stays vibrant and balanced. These living organisms influence everything from digestion and immunity to your emotional state. The yogis understood this long before microscopes existed. They saw that food is frequency. The vibration of what you consume directly affects the vibration of your Consciousness. Dense food creates a dense state of being. Light food creates lightness within you.

The *Ajna*, located between the eyebrows, is the subtle energy center that corresponds to the pineal gland. In yogic understanding, this gland is seen as the bridge between the physical and the spiritual, the eye of insight, the seat of intuitive perception. The pineal gland is the most important gland in your entire body. It's what's referred to as the third eye. Sugarcane and fluoride calcify the pineal gland and make it extremely dense. The more decalcified your pineal gland is, the faster it vibrates. The faster it vibrates, the more you're able to perceive, and the higher frequencies you're able to tune into.

The pineal gland is considered the doorway for all spirituality. It's like the antenna where your body, your machine, receives the broadcast of Consciousness. It naturally produces dimethyltryptamine (DMT), often called the Spirit Molecule, a compound that generates the visionary states many experience in deep meditation, lucid dreaming, and near-death experiences. Plant medicines such as psilocybin mushrooms and ayahuasca can temporarily open a floodgate of perception, activating deeper states of awareness. Yet this is only temporary. You don't need plant medicine to experience it. By becoming more conscious through meditation, conscious breathing, and clean eating, you can naturally activate the pineal gland and open the gateway to higher Consciousness from within.

Scientifically, the pineal gland is a small endocrine gland located near the center of the brain. It plays a vital role in regulating the body's circadian rhythm, the natural cycle of waking and sleeping. It does this by secreting the hormone melatonin, which rises in darkness and decreases when exposed to light. The pineal gland receives signals from the eyes through the sympathetic nervous system, converting serotonin into melatonin at night to guide the body into rest and repair. This rhythmic release of melatonin acts as a timekeeper for the entire system, synchronizing sleep patterns, body temperature, and hormone cycles with the movement of the sun.

I remember one day when I went to the grocery store. I'd spend hours going through the aisles, not sure what I should eat or what my body was calling for. I never used my phone or looked up what foods were considered healthy. I was guided purely by Spirit, by my intuition, my Higher Self. I'd spend hours walking up and down the aisles, holding the food, touching it, communicating with it, trying to discern what my body was truly asking for as I continued to heal myself naturally.

After a couple of hours, I grabbed a few things and went to

the cash register. The cashier tried to run my card a half dozen times, but it wouldn't work. I could've paid with cash, but I knew something deeper was happening. I intuitively felt that the Universe was trying to tell me something. The items I'd chosen weren't in full alignment with what my body needed in that moment, so the Universe blocked the transaction. I put the food back on the shelves and walked through the aisles again, letting my awareness guide me. I picked up different foods, the ones that felt lighter, cleaner, more aligned. When I returned to the same cashier working at the same register and used the same card, it went through immediately. I smiled. Once again, my Higher Self, the highest form of my intelligence, manifested this circumstance to teach me how to surrender, to accept what is without resistance, and to trust the subtle guidance always present beneath the noise of the mind. We're constantly being guided like this. The question is, are you still enough within yourself to perceive it? Is your mind quiet enough to hear it?

When I began eating only positive *Pranic* foods, *Sattvic* foods like pineapple, tangerines, and clementines, each bite sent waves of endorphins and euphoria coursing through me. It felt as though my entire being was dissolving into pure, boundless ecstasy. It was pure bliss. My awareness expanded beyond the physical realm. My intuition shone with crystal clarity. I noticed that when I ate foods low in *Prana*, my energy dimmed, my perception dulled, and my awareness contracted. It became effortless to choose the foods that brought me bliss because they amplified my vibration and enhanced my perception. They weren't exotic or complex. They were simple, natural, and alive, and they elevated every dimension of my being.

As my awareness deepened, food stopped being about nutrition and became about vibration. Each bite, each fast, was teaching me something about energy. I didn't plan to fast for long, it just started happening naturally. My body wanted space to cleanse, to reset, to awaken something deeper inside me.

Another important thing about food is it's not only important what you eat, but also how you eat and how often you eat. When we don't eat with the proper gaps in between each meal, it's constantly fueling the body, and it doesn't allow the body to go into its natural repair mode. The longer that you go in between meals without snacking, the longer you go in between eating anything, the more you're giving your body time to enter the repair mode and to do the repairs that are necessary. A major problem that people have is not only that they're eating the wrong types of food that the body needs to perform optimally, but that they're eating way too often. They're constantly snacking, and on a subconscious level they're having millions of actions being performed all the time because their digestive system is always active. It's not until your digestive system can be inactive due to you waiting a long enough time after eating that your body can go into the natural regenerative repair mode that's needed for cell regeneration.

Ideally we should wait at least six to eight hours in between meals. I personally only eat two meals a day, most of the time only one meal. When I'm living in my car I only eat dinner, and it's because I'm doing my breathing exercises all day while I'm driving, breathing from my diaphragm like I describe in another transmission. To do that type of breathing technique it's absolutely important to practice it on an empty stomach, so I intentionally only eat one meal a day so I can consciously breathe from the diaphragm doing that breathing technique, because that technique is very powerful. What I'm essentially doing is what science calls intermittent fasting. Intermittent fasting is when you go at least sixteen to eighteen hours from one meal to another, giving your body a longer rest period between meals. Modern research shows that fasting periods of fourteen to twenty hours allow the body to switch from burning glucose to burning stored fat for energy, lowering insulin levels and activating cellular repair processes known as autophagy. When you do this, it's extremely beneficial for your body and your mind. A big reason why people have so much mental diarrhea, so many compulsive thought patterns they don't prefer, is that they're eating way too often, and what they eat contributes directly to this. The cleaner you eat, the more natural foods, the less mental chatter you'll have. Your mind will be at ease, you'll be calmer. The more time you wait in between meals and the healthier you eat, the cleaner you eat, the more your system can restore itself.

When you allow sixteen to eighteen hours in between meals you're allowing the body to fully enter the natural healing mode of cell regeneration. You're allowing the body to clear out all the damaged protein cells and regenerate new ones. This process is what science refers to as autophagy, which literally means self-eating, a natural cleansing cycle that removes waste and promotes renewal. This is super important. Also, when you put your body in shock like that, like when you take a cold shower or when you push beyond the limitation of your body where your stomach feels like you're hungry but you choose not to eat, you're creating a mild stress known as hormesis. That mild stress teaches the body to adapt and grow stronger. It strengthens the nervous system and awakens new pathways in the brain. It's very important to do those things, to keep expanding the neural pathways in your brain and to allow the body to go into its natural healing and regeneration processes.

When I was going through my transformational process, when I quit the drugs and before my *Samadhi*, my body was going through something I didn't understand. I had no idea what was happening with me. My stomach would tighten up like a knot and I had so much energy even though I wasn't eating and even though I was coming off all these hardcore narcotics that I had been injecting into my veins. I went a week without eating or sleeping and I never stopped moving. Even when I lay down, my body kept shaking. My legs bounced uncontrollably, and no matter how hard I tried, I couldn't stop them. The energy moving through me was unlike anything I had ever experienced. It was as if something greater had taken control of my body, guiding every breath and every motion. Whatever my Higher Self told me to act on in every given moment, I willingly did it. I found out afterwards what was happening. By me acting on my highest excitement in every moment, by choosing to stay in a positive, pleasant state, and dissolve all the limiting negative fear-based beliefs in every given moment, I was raising my vibration. I was expanding, and by doing that it was actually giving me energy, true energy, *Prana*, not the chemical energy from food.

I couldn't understand how my physical body was able to have this type of stamina, this type of endurance, to push beyond the limitations of my body and mind, breaking through everything I once believed was possible. The last time I got off the needle and quit the drugs, cold turkey, when I was twenty-five, my body was so trashed that for months I could barely do anything. I could barely move. I had to lay in the fetal position and still take pharmaceuticals for my stomach because it was so messed up from all the drugs. Usually coming off opiates is debilitating. The body is in so much pain. You have absolutely no energy. You can't move, can't eat, can't sleep. You have diarrhea, vomiting, hot and cold sweats, and it's absolute misery. There are many suicides linked to the withdrawal of opiates because it's that excruciatingly painful.

This time, coming off the drugs again cold turkey, with my tolerance way higher than it had ever been before, I should've experienced even worse withdrawal symptoms than when I was twenty-five. Yet I didn't experience any of them. My stomach was completely fine. I didn't have diarrhea or vomiting. I did go through hot and cold sweats, which were part of the natural detoxification, but it wasn't nearly as uncomfortable as before. I didn't eat or sleep, but I wasn't fatigued. I had enormous amounts of energy, more than I had ever experienced before.

My body was constantly upgrading because I was raising my frequency, acting on my highest excitement, following my bliss in every given moment. I was literally tapping into pure life force energy and that's what was sustaining me. My *Kundalini* energy was ascending. I didn't need chemical food. When I finally tried to eat after several days, I took one bite and immediately my stomach locked up into a knot and I couldn't swallow it. It was like my body's own natural way of telling me, "Don't put food in me right now. We're in a purification process. We're in a cleansing process. Don't put any more toxins into me." Even healthy food still carries a small level of toxins, and my body was going through a complete purification process, ridding itself of all the chemicals from the drugs, all the toxins from the food, everything I had been putting into my body my whole life. It was going through an extremely rapid detoxification and purification process, not only on a chemical level but on an energetic and vibrational level as well. It was extremely intense and overwhelming, but I kept following the guidance of my Higher Self by following my bliss. I knew that even though my body hurt and I was tired physically, I had to keep pushing through, and every time I did, every time I broke another limitation, it gave me more energy instead of less. That's what allowed me to keep acting on my bliss instead of falling down and falling asleep. There was no way I could have slept even if I wanted to. My physical body may have been tired at moments from breaking all these limitations, but it literally would not stop moving. The energy coursing through me was unstoppable, alive, and expanding beyond anything I had ever known.

I went a week without eating or sleeping, and once my body was purified on a chemical level, physical level, and also on an energetic and vibrational level, that was when I was able to fall into *Samadhi* and experience a profound remembrance of truth and unity. That experience showed me that nourishment doesn't just come from food. It comes from alignment with Source itself. When you follow your bliss without fear, your body begins to live on that energy. Bliss nourishes the body, mind, and Soul all at once. Fasting became another form of feasting, a communion with life itself.

I'm not here to convince you what to eat. I'm inviting you to notice the state of being that different foods create. When I started becoming more conscious and my perception and awareness within myself were rising, I began to perceive biofeedback communicating directly through my body, showing me what I should and shouldn't eat. I've got fair skin and red hair, and throughout my life I could never stay in the sun for more than twenty minutes without getting sunburned and peeling back to white again. But after my transformation and *Samadhi* experiences, and after I started eating consciously and clean, I noticed I no longer got sunburned like before. I could actually tan. When I did burn, it never hurt. People would ask me how I could be so red and not be in pain, and I didn't have an answer. One evening my mom made her famous homemade tacos with meat, cheese, and her salsa that I'd always loved. I felt intuitively that I shouldn't eat them because of the meat, but I ignored it and enjoyed them anyway. That night as I lay in bed, my legs, which had been in the sun all day without pain, suddenly started burning intensely, like fire from within. It was unlike any sensation I'd ever felt. In that moment I knew exactly what it meant. It was my body's biofeedback telling me that the meat was lowering my vibration and creating internal resistance. I said to myself, alright, I get the message. No more meat.

Not long after that, my hand, while automatic writing, wrote the message: eat fruit today and only eat fruit today and see what happens. So I did. For several days the same message came through. I lived only on pineapple, five small bites a day. I'd never felt such radiant clarity and vitality moving through me in all my years. My energy was boundless, expanding with every breath. I could sit in complete stillness for hours without a single thought forming in my mind. My awareness and focus were sharper than ever. A few days later, I crashed my bicycle doing a wheelie and tore the skin completely off my left knee. I didn't even feel my skin being torn off my knee when I crashed. I had no idea I was bleeding until I looked down and saw blood pouring from my knee. My intuition told me to go into the lake and wash it off, so I did, against my mom's advice. She told me the lake was filthy and would cause infection. She was right. It became severely infected, but I refused medical attention, yet again. I didn't use soap, antibiotic cream, or anything else. This was also the time when I stopped showering in cities because of the chemicals in the water. I'd only bathe in lakes or in the shower at my mother's house because she had well water. This was yet again another circumstance beautifully orchestrated by my Higher Self to give me another opportunity to learn how to fully surrender and trust the highest form of my intelligence. While living only on pineapple, I noticed how beautifully the wound on my knee was healing. When I compared the scar on my left knee to the ones on my right arm, where the infected sores from injecting speedballs of heroin and cocaine had been, the difference was astonishing. When I healed my arms, I'd been living on Oreos and Frosted Flakes, pure sugarcane. When I healed my knee, I was living on fruit. You can still see the dark purple injection scars on my arm, but the wound on my knee is barely visible.

After about a month of living only on pineapple, my automatic writing told me, eat regular food again if you want. So I went with my mom to Panera Bread. As we stood in line, I looked at the menu. My awareness moved to the Fuji Apple Salad, but then drifted toward the Buffalo Chicken Ranch Melt that I used to love. In that exact moment, the wound on my left knee began burning like a torch had been set to it. Instantly I knew what my body was telling me. "Don't put that meat into our body while we're still healing." I shifted my awareness back to the salad, and the burning stopped immediately. That moment was profoundly revealing. My body was communicating directly with my conscious thought, showing me in real time how intention and biology are connected. I realized that what I was perceiving was the subconscious mind, the operating system of the body, sending immediate biofeedback to my conscious awareness. I was simultaneously perceiving both the conscious and the subconscious, the two hemispheres of my own intelligence communicating as one. Most people never experience this because subconscious brainwave activity typically remains hidden beneath waking awareness. Yet in that moment, I could perceive multiple brainwave frequencies at once, the waking and the subconscious in perfect coherence. It was clear that this was guidance from the higher form of my intelligence, reminding me not to act out of compulsiveness, but from alignment. That moment forever changed how I understood the dialogue between my subconscious and conscious mind.

I was already fighting off a major bacterial infection in my knee. I was using all of my energy to heal myself, and if I'd eaten the meat, it would've taken a lot of my energy away from healing just to digest the food itself. I found out afterwards that consuming meat takes seventy-two hours to run through your entire system. What happens if you leave a piece of meat out on the counter for three days? It starts to rot and spoil, yes? Now imagine what's happening to the meat within the body. The body is like a hot oven, a breeding ground for bacteria. The body must produce tons of antibodies in order to fight off the bacteria from the meat. If I would've eaten the meat that day, I would've been exerting tremendous energy producing antibodies that would've been redirected to the bacteria on the meat instead of healing the bacterial infection within my knee.

Another sensation I've noticed within my body is that if I eat sugarcane or any kind of refined sugar that doesn't come from fruit, my left arm starts to itch intensely. It's not a surface itch, it's deep within the arm itself. This happens whenever I eat junk food or anything unnatural. It's more biofeedback. My body is telling me, don't put this into my body right now. This isn't good for you, and I've learned to listen to my body and trust the highest form of my intelligence. I've learned to eat consciously, to listen to what my body calls for and what it needs to run optimally so that my perception stays high, so that my vibration stays high, because that's the only thing that truly matters. The more radiant your *Pranamaya Kosha* becomes, the more effortlessly the physical body aligns with it. This is how we heal ourselves. Doctors don't tell you this because they don't understand it. Doctors focus on the physical body. They focus on symptoms and treat the body, not the root. The root is in the energy body, the metaphysical dimension of you. We're multi-dimensional beings. The physical body is simply the most dense part of our being. If we take care of our energy body, if we keep it vibrant and radiant, the physical body will heal itself from all ailments. Through *Samadhi*, I realized how healing happens from within.

So again, I'm not here to tell you what to eat. You can eat whatever you want, just do it consciously. The more conscious you become, the more biofeedback you'll perceive within your body, your vehicle that holds Consciousness into physical form. It'll communicate to you and tell you exactly what you need to know. Eating consciously is extremely important. It should always be done in silence with full awareness in the present moment so you can pay attention to and perceive all of the subtle biofeedback. Another indicator that I've learned to discern from my body is that it doesn't matter what I'm eating, when I've had enough, my left nostril starts to run. It's not from spice or heat, it's simply the signal that my body has had enough to function optimally right now. When this happens, I stop eating. That's how I know my energy is balanced and I'm not overexerting energy digesting unnecessary food. I treat my body like the valuable high-performance machine that it is, much like a race car. Race cars, particularly in series like Formula One , don't fill their tanks completely. Instead, they're filled with the minimum amount of fuel needed to finish the race, minimizing weight and maximizing speed. Eating consciously means chewing your food thoroughly, counting each chew at least twenty-four times per each morsel of food. This practice anchors you in the now, keeps you present, and aware of what and how you're eating. Before I eat, I give thanks and gratitude for the food for giving its life to sustain mine. Before I drink water, I give thanks and gratitude to the water for sustaining my body so I can continue this human experience. The food and water begin to work differently within you when you eat consciously and treat it as sacred communing, not consumption.

As I've said before, gratitude is the second highest frequency. The more you practice it in every given moment, the more aware you become within the moment and the more you anchor your awareness in the ever-expanding now, the more you will maintain your vibration in the second highest frequency of gratitude indefinitely. The more aware you become within yourself, the more biofeedback you're able to perceive, and the more you realize that your Higher Self is always communicating through your physical body. Your body will literally tell you everything you need to know. The only question is, are you paying enough attention to perceive it? Are you able to maintain your awareness in the present moment long enough to discern what these sensations in your body mean?

Most people can't do this. Most people have so much mental chatter constantly playing in their mind, compulsive thoughts looping between memory and imagination, that they don't even notice the subtle sensations within their body. They're not even aware they're happening, let alone able to be curious about them.

CLOSING REFLECTION

Eating consciously isn't about following rules or restrictions. It's about being fully present with what you're putting into your body and how it feels when you do. Your body is always talking to you. It's always giving you biofeedback, showing you what raises your vibration and what lowers it. Most people simply aren't paying attention long enough to notice.

When you listen, really listen, you'll start to realize that your Higher Self communicates through every sensation, every subtle change within you. What you put into your body becomes what you experience through your mind. The cleaner you eat, the sharper your perception becomes.

Food isn't just food. It's frequency. It's *Prana*. It's Consciousness taking physical form so that you can experience yourself through this human machine. If you eat with full awareness, with gratitude for every bite, your vibration will rise naturally. You'll start to feel lighter, clearer, and more alive than you ever thought possible.

Eat consciously. Listen deeply. Give thanks for every meal. Let every bite remind you that you're not just feeding a body, you're feeding the divine that lives within you.

TRANSMISSION 6

THE HIGHER SELF SPEAKS

When I began to listen beyond my mind, I realized that my Higher Self had been speaking to me all along through every feeling, every sign, and every circumstance I once thought was coincidence.

When I was going through my transformation, I started noticing a profound wave of synchronicities. Synchronicities don't just happen as 11:11 on the clock or 3:33 in the afternoon. They're not coincidences; they are the organizing principle of reality. The more synchronicities you experience, the more clearly the Universe shows you that your internal world is coming into alignment, since your outer world always reflects your inner world.

I was going through such rapid transformation that my outer world looked like it was burning down around me. My drug business was collapsing, my old life was dissolving, and my friends and family all thought I was losing my mind. Everyone wrote me off except for my mother, bless her heart.

She was the only one who stayed by my side through it all. I understood why everyone else pulled away. People fear what they don't understand, and all separation stems from fear. Every form of judgment and discrimination arises from fear. I didn't let it bother me. I knew everything that was happening was meant to happen exactly as it was. I intuitively understood that I had chosen all of it to teach me how to transcend fear. One of those fears was the fear of being alone. I had to learn to be completely alone and realize through *Samadhi* that I am never alone, because I literally am All That Is. All separation is an illusion.

One of the most important lessons my Higher Self taught me was how to completely surrender. A major reason my transformation was so fast and my inner alignment happened so rapidly was that I removed the word *no* from my vocabulary. I lived as yes and yes to everything. It didn't matter what came through, whether it was a thought in my mind, a sensation in my body, or words my hand wrote through automatic writing. I stayed fluid and said yes. Removing *no* got me entirely out of my own way. It allowed me to surrender fully to the highest form of my intelligence, my Higher Self. Saying yes to everything removes resistance. It allows life to unfold exactly as it's meant to. When you stop trying to control reality, you start trusting it. You begin to see that everything is happening in Divine Order.

Living as yes and yes brought me into circumstances that in the past I never would've agreed to face. Through those experiences, I learned to remain in a positive and pleasant state no matter what. I stopped forming opinions about life. I no longer labeled things as good or bad, right or wrong, or decided what I liked and didn't like. I stayed neutral, exuding gratitude for whatever was unfolding in the moment. This dissolved belief systems that had kept me trapped. I began dissolving every unconscious belief that had once defined who I thought I was. I realized I could consciously choose how I wanted to be in every given moment. I could choose my state of being, my frequency. Standing at death's doorstep taught me that tomorrow isn't promised. My father's sudden passing moments after I spoke to him on the phone reminded me that even the next moment isn't promised. All I had was this one, the ever-expanding now. Since the only moment that truly exists is now, I chose to live in bliss within it. I chose to live consciously, moment by moment, breath by breath. Everything I share comes down to this simple truth: conscious choice. Every transmission in this book leads back to that. When you become conscious enough, you realize you choose your state of being in every given moment. You no longer have to react from fear or act on compulsive thought patterns created by unconscious beliefs. You can choose consciously.

Every circumstance is neutral. It isn't good or bad, positive or negative. It's simply neutral. The meaning you assign to it gives it charge. Your beliefs give it energy. When you stop labeling things and stop forming opinions, you stop creating new belief systems. When you stop identifying with anything, the ego begins to dissolve. The more you identify with, the more you suffer. The more you attach to, the more conflict arises within you, and the stronger the illusion of separation feels from Source. Letting go of opinion and judgment frees you. Gratitude naturally fills the space where resistance once lived, and miracles begin to unfold effortlessly. Life becomes lighter. Circumstances may look the same, but your perception changes, and perception is everything.

One of the greatest lessons my Higher Self ever taught me came through automatic writing. At the time, my business was falling apart. The drug trade I had built my life around was collapsing. I'd been robbed, people owed me large sums of money, and I had no idea how to repay my main connection, a man we'll call George. I met George through another friend and business partner, who we'll call Bob. I paid Bob five thousand dollars for the introduction, and George paid Bob five thousand as well. On the way to meet George, Bob said, "Don't mess with George's money. He's a good guy, but he's killed people for less." I laughed it off, thinking, don't be ridiculous. I'd never mess with his money. Yet that statement turned out to be important because it painted the backdrop for what came next.

After I was robbed, I owed George over forty thousand dollars. Fear began creeping in. He called me every day, and I ignored every call. I didn't know what to say. Then one day, my hand wrote several times during automatic writing, go tell George the truth. He'll understand. Go tell George the truth. He'll understand. When I came out of the trance and read the words, I knew immediately what I had to do. It was another test. My Higher Self wanted me to surrender completely. I wasn't sure if I'd walk out of his house alive. I thought about calling or texting my mom to say goodbye, but I didn't. I fully surrendered and once again accepted that if this is the way I'm supposed to die, then so be it. I didn't call George. I got in my car, drove to his house, walked straight in the door like I owned the place, and went directly to his office. He was sitting at his computer. I stood in front of him and said, "George, I'm so sorry. I messed up your money." He stood up from his chair. I wasn't sure what was about to happen. I didn't know if I was about to get shot or beaten. I stayed completely present, breathing calmly, watching him. Instead of anger, he walked toward me and wrapped his arms around me. This man, known for his strength and intensity, embraced me fully with both arms. I could feel his heart against mine. There was no anger, no tension, no fear. Only love. Pure, unconditional love radiating through his body into mine. Then he said softly, "Red, don't ever let money come between us." In that moment, I realized what was happening. This wasn't about dissolving fear.

There was no fear left to dissolve. It was confirmation of the frequency I had chosen to live in, total surrender, trust, and love. Since I had already transcended the fear before walking in, the outer world reflected it perfectly back to me. The hug wasn't what made me fearless. The hug was the proof of what fearlessness creates.

As we sat down, I told him everything, my *Kundalini* awakening, my *Samadhi* experiences, the realization of unity with Source. He smiled at me with that same knowing look, eyes soft and calm. The way he looked at me said everything. It was as if he were telling me telepathically, "Red, it's about time you figured this out. I've been waiting for you to remember." He didn't say it physically, but I could feel it psychically through the connection that had opened between us. While we were sitting there, he turned slightly in his chair, grabbed a piece of paper from his desk, and began to write. When he handed it to me, I saw that it looked exactly like my automatic writing, chicken scratch, barely legible, yet radiating with energy. What he wrote was exactly what I needed to hear for the next steps of my life. It was as if he had known this was going to happen all along, maybe not consciously, but on a deeper level. Consciousness was flowing through him, showing me that I was exactly where I was meant to be.

He forgave my entire debt on the spot. He said, "I could shake your hand right now and never see you again, and I'd still have nothing but love and respect for you." That moment changed me forever. The last person I ever expected to understand me was the only one who did. Once again, it was a perfect circumstance manifested by my Higher Self to teach me how to transcend fear, stay out of imagination, stay in the now, and master my state of being no matter what was happening.

Every single time I faced fear with total surrender, my awareness expanded. Each time I stayed present and didn't resist, I became lighter. The Universe was showing me again and again that circumstances don't matter. Only my state of being matters. Only my frequency. I was learning how to perceive the subtle sensations in my body and recognize how my Higher Self communicated with me through them. I would sit perfectly still for hours, unmoving, totally thoughtless, resting in awareness. Sometimes thoughts would arise, but they weren't intentional and they weren't compulsive. They came in the form of questions, and since I had already decided to live as yes and yes, whatever question appeared, I automatically knew I would say yes. What I began noticing was that each yes carried a subtle physical response, a kind of biofeedback that my body would give me. It wasn't like electricity or static; it was very soft and subtle, something most people would miss entirely if they weren't still enough to notice it. These sensations became my inner language with my Higher Self. They were how my higher intelligence communicated through my physical body.

By being yes and yes, it gave me a baseline to learn how to perceive and discern the biofeedback that my Higher Self constantly communicates through the body. I would sit either with my eyes open or closed, completely aware of every breath, and if I felt an itch or a twinge in my body, I wouldn't react. I wouldn't scratch it or move away from it. I would just observe and ask myself, what thought was I just having in this exact moment? What was I feeling? What is my higher intelligence communicating to me through this? One clear signal that I've been able to discern within my body is when something is a resounding yes. My right leg or my right foot will give off this subtle tingling or twinging sensation. It's very gentle and precise, but I know exactly what it means. It's my Higher Self saying, keep your foot on the gas. That's how I know it's a full-body yes, a confirmation to move forward immediately without hesitation.

One day, while sitting on my couch in that stillness, I had

the thought that my neighbor was about to get home and that I should go hold the door open for him. I didn't know where the thought came from, but I trusted it. I stood up, walked outside, and at that exact moment, he was pulling into the driveway. I held the door open and said, "Hey, I've got to tell you something." I told him that a few weeks before, when he asked me at four in the morning if I was high, I'd lied to him and said no, even though I was. I told him I'd been injecting speedballs but that I'd quit cold turkey and had been experiencing things I couldn't explain. I showed him my arm and told him that I was in the process of healing myself. He looked at me, not judging, not shocked, just present. Then he began to speak, but it wasn't him speaking anymore. Consciousness was channeling directly through him. He went into this flow state, pouring out words that were perfectly tailored to me. His mouth moved, but the words I heard didn't match what his lips were forming. It was as if I was hearing a higher frequency translation. Every word he said answered every question that had been forming in my mind before he arrived.

One of the things that he told me was, "Don't let anything have control over you, not money, not drugs, not cigarettes, not alcohol, not anyone or anything. Be completely free." In that moment, I was smoking a cigarette, and when I heard those words, I understood completely. I put it out right there on the ground, hugged him, and said, "Thank you for those words. I truly appreciate you. I have nothing but love for you." He hugged me back, and the vibration that moved through both of us was beyond words, waves of bliss moving in both directions, two beings harmonizing in perfect resonance.

After I put the cigarette out, I went back inside and sat on the couch, meditating again for a while. A few hours passed, and I thought to myself, you know what, I can do whatever I want. If I want to smoke a cigarette, I can smoke a cigarette. I had no limiting belief that I couldn't or shouldn't do something.

My whole life, I'd always done whatever I wanted, never believing that I couldn't. So I said, alright, I'm going to go smoke a cigarette. I walked outside, lit the cigarette, took one puff, and immediately felt like I was going to die. I'd never experienced a heart attack before, but what I felt must've been close. Yet it wasn't exactly that. It was energy swirling violently around my *Anahata*. My heart was pounding, but beyond the heartbeat, I could literally feel the *Prana* spinning around my chest like a vortex.

I flicked the cigarette away and used every bit of my awareness to stay focused in the present moment. It was yet another divine circumstance my Higher Self created to help me transcend fear. I walked back toward my apartment, fully conscious of every step, every breath. I watched the cracks in the pavement, the texture of the carpet on the stairs, the way my foot pressed into it with each step. I anchored my awareness into every detail so that my mind wouldn't drift into imagination.

When I made it back inside, I sat down in the living room and meditated for twenty or thirty minutes. Slowly, my heart calmed down. The energy around my *Anahata* softened and became gentle again. I could still feel it swirling, but it was becoming more subtle and balanced.

Then I went to my bedroom, sat down, and played *Isha Kriya*, the guided meditation I'd mentioned earlier. It lasted about twelve minutes. When it ended, everything in me returned to stillness. My energy was centered again. Afterward, I picked up the cigarette pack, crumpled it in my hand, and threw it in the trash. I never smoked another cigarette again. My body had become extremely sensitive to stimulants, to food, to energy, to everything. My awareness was beyond measure. Every sensation, every subtle pulse of energy in my body was communicating to me what I should or shouldn't put into it. Whenever my Higher Self had something to show me, it would often use the body as its messenger. Each experience was dramatic, intense, and unforgettable because that's what it took to get through to me. My circumstances are my school, teaching me how to master my state of being, just like your circumstances are your school, giving you the opportunity to learn to master yours as well. I was stubborn, so I often had to manifest the same lesson multiple times before it fully sank in. But I wouldn't change any of it. Every single experience expanded my awareness, bringing me closer to freedom and liberation.

This is how I began learning to interpret the language of the body. Every time I stayed still long enough, I could feel more. The more still I became, the more awareness I had of every subtle sensation and every shift of energy within me. I started realizing that these physical cues weren't random. They were direct communication from Consciousness itself, using the body as a vehicle to translate vibration into perception. Eventually, this became second nature; when I would go stay with other people, my presence would naturally begin to shift the energy in the space, helping to raise their vibration through resonance alone. Even when they weren't consciously aware of it, I could feel their frequency rising, and I'd always know when it was time to leave. I'd feel this subtle tingling in my left arm. The moment I felt it, I knew I'd completed what I came there to do and that it was time to move on. I'd pack up and be gone by the next morning. My Higher Self guided every step of the way, moment by moment, through these subtle sensations and synchronicities.

Another way the Higher Self communicates is through external synchronicities in the world. Since all separation is an illusion, my Higher Self and your Higher Self are both expressions of the same Higher Mind. Nothing happens by accident. Nothing is random. Everything is perfectly choreographed, like a divine symphony of vibration unfolding in real time. I used to sit on the couch for hours, staring out the window in absolute stillness, not moving, simply observing life as it passed by. My awareness was fully present in every breath, every flicker of light, every sound. When a thought appeared, I knew it was significant, because thoughts no longer arose out of compulsion. Each one had purpose.

One day, a thought formed in my mind that said, go to Sedona. In that exact moment, a man walking his dog passed by the window wearing a shirt that said Arizona across the front. I laughed out loud, realizing the synchronicity. My Higher Self was literally answering me through the external world. Things like that started happening constantly. I used to write them all down in a three-ring binder. Within a few months, I'd filled the entire thing. I remember once sitting there thinking, what are the odds? How could every single thought I have be immediately answered by something in my environment, whether it's a stranger's words, a billboard, a song lyric, an animal, an insect, or even the timing of a random sound? Then I realized there were no odds. It wasn't random. It was all orchestrated by Consciousness, perfectly designed for me. I wasn't just living in the Universe. The Universe was living through me.

Music became another medium for communication. When I needed guidance or deeper understanding, I'd let my phone shuffle through random songs. I never chose a playlist, never searched for anything specific. I'd just sit there in stillness, not expecting anything, not thinking, but aware. As thoughts or questions formed in my mind, the lyrics would immediately respond word for word, answering me in perfect timing. It was like having a psychic conversation with the Universe through music. Every song, every line, was tailor made for me. It was the same Consciousness speaking through different channels such as music, numbers, people, words, colors, and symbols, all of it in perfect harmony.

Music became a powerful way to keep my awareness anchored in the now. When you listen deeply, not just with your ears but with your whole being, you can feel the vibration of every note moving through you. It sharpens the mind and expands perception. When you stop drifting into memory or imagination and listen with full presence, the now opens into infinity. That's when life stops feeling like coincidence and starts revealing itself as a living reflection of your vibration. Once you reach that level of awareness, your life becomes effortless to navigate. You realize there's no such thing as luck or chance. Everything is intelligence communicating with itself through the illusion of form. You're never a victim of anything. You're the creator of it all, orchestrating it from higher planes of awareness.

When people are caught in victim consciousness, they can't see this. They label things as unfair or traumatic. They think life is happening to them instead of for them. But every challenge is Consciousness showing you where fear still lives. Every circumstance is a mirror designed to help you evolve and expand. When you realize this, you stop resisting life. You begin to see the hidden perfection in everything. You start to understand that every synchronicity, every sensation, every event is a message from the highest form of intelligence, your Higher Self, reminding you that you're never separate from Source. You are Source, playing the human game of remembering itself.

There were times when the communication became even more obvious, more tangible. Poltergeist activity started happening around me. Electronics began acting strange, reacting to my thoughts and emotions as if they were alive. Lights flickered. Songs started playing on their own. My phone would turn on by itself, even when it was across the room, and it would open a random video or song that perfectly answered whatever I was thinking about in that exact moment. It felt as though Consciousness was having a direct conversation with me through technology. My phone became like a living extension of my energy field, responding instantly to the vibration of my thoughts. It reminded me of the way Bumblebee communicates in the movie *Transformers*, scanning through radio stations to form sentences. That's what it felt like. My Higher Self was using any medium available to speak to me, and at that time, digital signals were the easiest path. Psychic information always follows the path of least resistance.

These experiences happened so often that they became normal. The line between the physical and nonphysical blurred completely. My outer reality was reflecting every movement of my inner vibration. I understood that what people call paranormal is simply perception expanding beyond the limits of the five senses. It's not strange or supernatural. It's natural. It's what happens when the walls between dimensions grow thin and the illusion of separation dissolves. Most people don't understand this kind of thing, and that's perfectly fine. They don't need to. My experience is tailor made for me, just like your experience is tailor made for you. The Universe speaks to each of us in a language only we can understand. Everything that happens is a reflection of our unique vibration, perfectly designed by the Higher Mind that we all share.

When I emerged from a five-hour *Samadhi* state and opened my eyes, it felt as though only fifteen minutes had passed. That experience shifted something permanently within me. It felt like my Consciousness had ascended in frequency into a higher density of awareness. When I opened my eyes, I no longer felt even the slightest trace of separation or division. I was everything I perceived, and everything I perceived was me. The boundary between what was me and what wasn't me dissolved completely. Everything is me. I was total stillness, total emptiness. No thoughts, no beliefs, no opinions, no identity. Just pure bliss radiating from the center of my being in every direction.

Nothing I'd ever experienced through drugs could compare

to this, and I'd taken them all in large amounts. This is beyond anything the mind can compare to. I could feel that I was the entire Universe, the very vibration animating all form. I realized that everything is made of the same energy that I was, the same Consciousness vibrating at different frequencies. I was no longer the one perceiving energy. I was energy itself. I no longer identified with the physical body and became everything. I am the vast infinite ocean of intelligence, Source, choosing to experience itself through this human form. Identification was no longer possible because there was nothing left to identify with. What remained was the realization itself, awakening within the dream we call physical reality and seeing it for what it truly is, a living simulation of vibration, a reflection of Consciousness expressing itself through physical form.

Later that night, I stood in the parking lot of my apartment around two in the morning. The air was still, and the sky was crystal clear. Energy from the *Samadhi* state was overflowing through every cell of my body. Words can never truly convey what I felt. There was no separation between me and the stars above. I looked up and said out loud, "I know you're out there. If you're in the area, and if you don't mind, could you please show yourself to me? If not, it's okay. I understand." A few minutes went by, and just as I was about to walk inside, a craft materialized in the sky to my right. It floated silently across the horizon from right to left, completely black and metallic looking, with no lights, shaped almost like a hockey puck hovering in the sky. It moved slowly, effortlessly, as if it were gliding through water rather than air. Then it dematerialized right before my eyes.

When it vanished, I stood there in awe, flooded with bliss. I had no fear, no disbelief. Only absolute knowing. This was confirmation of what I'd already realized in *Samadhi*, that Consciousness is infinite and that there are other intelligences existing on frequencies beyond what most can perceive. I wasn't hallucinating. I could feel them communicating with me not just visually, but through vibration, emotion, and subtle energy.

I went back into my apartment too ecstatic to sleep. I felt waves of energy moving through me, higher and higher. I went into my bedroom listening to music, fully immersed in it. I was one hundred percent present in the moment, completely absorbed with my entire being. There were no thoughts, no memories, no imagination, only awareness and sound. I was in this state for hours, timeless, completely still inside.

Then I went to stand up, and in that moment, my whole body started violently convulsing and shaking. I didn't know what was happening. I thought maybe I was having a seizure. I wasn't sure, because I'd never had one before, so I jumped backward onto my bed and allowed my body to do whatever it needed to do. I surrendered completely and let the violent shaking and convulsing happen. It looked like a scene from *The Exorcist*. My body was shaking so hard that if I hadn't been on my bed, I would've broken things and definitely hurt myself. I couldn't stop it. I don't know if it lasted ten or fifteen minutes or several hours, because I was completely timeless.

As this was happening, my mouth suddenly opened. It felt like something was literally pulling my jaw apart. My mouth opened wider than I ever thought possible, and I couldn't control it. Even if I tried with all my strength to close it, I couldn't. My jaw was being forced open, and I started yawning, the biggest yawn of my entire life. It went on and on. Again, I had no sense of time. I was timeless. During this yawn, I could see white light coming out of my mouth and from the top of my head. As I was violently convulsing, with my eyes rolled back, it felt like a white beam of light was shooting through me, flowing out from my crown and my mouth at the same time. It reminded me of the scene from *The Fifth Element* when the woman looks up toward the light and her mouth opens, and that beam of energy pours out. That's how it felt. I could see it in my mind's eye.

Then I heard a collective of voices in my mind. It sounded like a group of women all speaking perfectly coherently at once, completely synchronized as one voice. It wasn't chaotic. It was unified. I could hear the voices clearly, but more than that, I could feel them. Every word they spoke carried waves of unconditional love. The feeling that washed through me was pure, boundless bliss. It wasn't just sound; it was an energetic, telepathic transmission of emotion. Their collective presence felt like Divine Mother, nurturing, infinite, and all-embracing. Even though my body was going through violent and intense convulsions that I couldn't control, I felt completely safe, held in the arms of something sacred. They kept repeating the same thing over and over: "Remember, remember, remember who you are." While this was happening, something beyond words took place. I received what I can only describe as a massive psychic download. It was like everything I needed to know about this life, my path, my purpose, my Soul, was revealed to me all at once. I remembered my Soul contract. I remembered why I chose this incarnation. I remembered that what I'm doing now in this life is a continuation of something I began long ago, in another lifetime, or more accurately, another parallel lifetime, because all of existence is taking place right now. It was the most profound experience of remembrance I'd ever had. I didn't read it or learn it. I remembered it. Every cell in my body knew it to be true.

I couldn't sleep that night. The energy surging through me was so intense I couldn't stay still. So as soon as the sun began to rise, I felt compelled to get in my car and start driving north toward Hugo.

CLOSING REFLECTION

Your Higher Self is always speaking to you. It speaks through sensation, intuition, synchronicity, and every circumstance you experience. The more silent you become within yourself, the clearer that communication becomes. When the mind stops chasing thoughts, when you no longer label or resist what arises, you begin to feel the subtle language of energy, the living dialogue between you and the infinite.

Every circumstance in your life is a mirror, a message, a reflection of your current frequency. When you choose to stay present, to respond with love instead of fear, you align with the intelligence that orchestrates all of creation. Guidance is no longer something you seek. It becomes the way you live.

Your Higher Self is not somewhere outside of you. It is you, the eternal Consciousness watching through your eyes, breathing through your breath, and guiding you home to the remembrance of truth and unity.

TRANSMISSION 7

THE MESSENGERS OF LIGHT

After that night, something within me shifted permanently. My awareness had touched infinity, and yet life kept revealing new ways to experience that infinite through form. What happened next showed me how Consciousness communicates through vibration, through synchronicity, and through the beings of light that guide us along the way.

I was compelled to drive to Hugo, Minnesota, about thirty minutes north of St. Paul, where I lived at the time. I had no plan, no map, no destination. I was simply following my intuition. I found myself driving out onto a farmer's field, completely surrounded by open land. I parked my car, stepped out, and felt that same overwhelming stillness and unity moving through me. I thought to myself, why am I here? Then I realized I was brought here for a reason. I looked up at the sky again and spoke out loud to the Universe, "I know you're out there. If you're in the area, can you please show yourself to me. If not, it's okay, but if you don't mind, I'd really love to see you."

Within moments, a dozen light orbs appeared in the air around me and my car, no more than twenty feet away. They moved gracefully in complete silence, swirling through the air in perfect synchronicity as if dancing with my frequency. It was beautiful. It was love. Once again, they showed themselves on command. I knew this was real, alive, intelligent, and loving beyond anything imagination could ever create. The connection I felt wasn't just visual; it was vibrational, emotional, telepathic. They were communicating not through words but through feeling. I could feel them speaking directly into my heart.

That night, I couldn't sleep again. The energy rushing through me was incredible. Later, as I sat in my apartment, I started seeing flashes in my mind's eye, images of arrows, bright and fast, pointing left or right. They came faster than the speed of light, appearing for an instant and vanishing. At first, I didn't realize what they meant. For a moment I wondered if I was going into psychosis, asking myself, is this my imagination, or is this something else coming through, some kind of communication. But I soon realized they were guiding me. I got in my car again, feeling compelled to follow the arrows. A left arrow would flash, and I'd turn left. Then a right arrow would appear, and I'd turn right. I followed this guidance until I ended up on a dead-end street. At the end of the road, there was a car with its headlights on. Fear crept in, and I thought, "I shouldn't be here. It's late. I need to leave." I turned around and started driving away. Then I heard a clear commanding voice in my mind saying, "Turn around." It wasn't my voice. It was calm but powerful, repeating over and over, "turn around, turn around, turn around." Now the image I was seeing in my mind's eye was no longer flashing. It became a steady, unbroken continuation of a U-turn symbol, like the U-turn signs they have in the United States. It didn't flicker anymore. It stayed constant, like the Universe was screaming at me to turn around, making sure

I couldn't miss the message because it was no longer subtle. It was overwhelming.

So I did. I turned the car around and drove back. The headlights were gone. I continued down the road and saw a large building in the woods, not a house, but something else. It had a small parking lot, so I parked and noticed a trail leading into the trees. I grabbed my journal and followed the path. It led me deep into the woods where I found a clearing and sat down. I closed my eyes and began to meditate. I went into another very deep meditative state, not as deep as the *Samadhi* state from the night before, but very deep nonetheless. The sensations in my body were intense. The only thing I can compare it to is being electrocuted with an electrical current, but it wasn't like that. It didn't hurt, but it had that same kind of strange tingling sensation moving through my entire body. I began to see streams of energy, different colors, geometric shapes, but I couldn't describe them. After a while, I opened my eyes and almost immediately, I felt that familiar surge of energy rising within me, and then my hand began to move on its own across the page. The words poured out faster than I could consciously think.

One of the first messages that came through said that higher forms of intelligence often communicate through the technology we already use, phones, radios, screens, even electrical currents. These are the bridges they can reach us through because they already exist within our collective frequency. It made me wonder if what I was experiencing all along was my Higher Self speaking through synchronicity, or if these beings were communicating through the very devices around me. Maybe it was both. Maybe it's all the same voice, the Higher Self, the Higher Mind, the same Consciousness using whatever medium is available to reach us. When I finished writing, I felt an immense wave of energy move through me, revealing even more of what I already was. I stood up and spoke out loud to the Universe, "I know you're out there, and if you're in the area, can you please show yourself to me. If not, it's okay, but if you don't mind, I'd really love to see you."

Moments later, the same craft appeared once more, the same black, metallic, hockey puck shaped object from the night before. It materialized right above the trees, glided silently across the sky, then faded into nothing. I looked around completely present, breathing deeply, feeling absolute bliss. The energy flooding through me was beyond anything words could ever describe. It wasn't calm or peaceful in the way people imagine peace. It was ecstatic. It was alive. Peace was simply the natural consequence of being in that much bliss. The sheer intensity of it was almost too much to contain. It felt like every atom in my body was exploding with light. I couldn't even comprehend how so much bliss could exist in a human form. It was insane, overwhelming, beautiful, and perfect all at once. I turned to walk back to my car and noticed a sign on the building nearby, Christos Spirituality Center. I smiled. In that instant, I knew this wasn't random. My Higher Self had guided me there through vibration, intuition, and trust. I realized this other intelligence, these beings, these lights, this presence, had been guiding me my entire life. That realization brought back a memory from my childhood that I will never forget.

When I was a child, no more than five years old, my family and I went to Taco Johns in my hometown of Hudson, Wisconsin, for dinner. It was pouring rain that day, raining so hard it looked like a wall of water. You'd be soaked just by running from the car to the front door of the restaurant. It was my father, my mother, my sister, and me. We went into Taco Johns and ordered our food. We sat at the corner booth we always sat at, the one by the window where you could see the main intersection. Across the street, my father noticed a man sitting there. He had no luggage and looked like he hadn't eaten in days. All he had were the clothes on his back. My father said he felt compelled to go out and speak with him. So he left my mother, sister, and me in the restaurant to continue eating while he walked out to the intersection to greet this man. They spoke for a while, and then my father handed him some money and came back in. I remember staring at this man through the window, in awe of him. I couldn't describe it or understand it then, but he had completely captured my attention.

We finished dinner and noticed that when we left, the man had left as well. My father said he saw him walk across the freeway, down the frontage road, toward the Hardee's that was maybe a quarter to a half mile away. We all assumed we were heading home, but instead, we somehow ended up pulling into the Hardee's parking lot. My father said he felt compelled to go there. He didn't know why. He couldn't explain it. He just felt drawn. We saw the man sitting inside by the window, all alone, with nothing in front of him but a cup of coffee. He had saved the money my father gave him, probably trying to make it last as long as possible, and ordered only a coffee to warm himself from the cold rain he'd been drenched in. My father left us in the car and went inside to talk with him. After some time, they both walked out together. They got into the car, and my father introduced him to us. His name was Steve. My father said this man was going to come stay with us for a while and live in our basement. Steve offered to help around the house, painting, staining the deck, simple things like that. In return, we'd feed him and give him a place to stay. He was an extremely kind man. You could see galaxies in his eyes. They were filled with compassion, and his heart radiated tenderness. My mother mentioned to some of the neighbors what had happened, that he was a homeless man we had taken in, and of course, out of their own fear and the stereotypes of what homeless people are, they were distant and cold toward him. That was their loss because this man was the embodiment of love.

He stayed with us for a while. I didn't remember much

about that time until decades later when everything started awakening within me again during my transformation. Suddenly, he began appearing in my memory more and more vividly. I'd ask my mother about him constantly regarding what she remembered about Steve. She'd ask why I wanted to know, and I'd tell her, "I'm not sure, but he keeps showing up in my mind, and I know he's significant. Tell me everything you remember." She told me that as a child, I had profound conversations with him, conversations no five year old should've been capable of. I asked him questions about the Universe, about outer space, Consciousness, and the stars, questions far beyond my age or understanding. The amazing thing was that Steve answered every single one with confidence and certainty. This was before the internet, long before Google existed, so there was no way my parents could verify what he was telling me. But they said they could feel the truth in his words. Even without understanding it, they somehow knew he was speaking from a place of knowing. Steve and I became very close. We shared many conversations like that. He was playful, wise, and carried an energy that brought peace into the house.

After about ten days, he told my parents it was time for him to go. When they asked where he wanted to be dropped off, he said the freeway on-ramp would be fine. At that time, Hudson, Wisconsin, was a small town. The on-ramp was surrounded by fields, grass as far as you could see, with no buildings or traffic around. My father pulled over, and we all said goodbye. Steve stepped out of the car and started walking toward the on-ramp. My father drove forward just a little, looked into the rearview mirror, and Steve was gone. He had vanished into thin air. There was nowhere he could've gone. It was an open field in every direction. He simply disappeared, like a being stepping between dimensions.

During my awakening, through automatic writing, I found out that Steve is deeply significant in my life, that he came to plant seeds of remembrance, keys that would activate years later when the time was right. Steve is a member of my Star Family. I always knew, or at least felt, that he wasn't from here in the ordinary sense. This guidance, whatever it was, whoever it was, has always been present in my life. I've felt it like a current just beneath the surface, shaping my path, guiding each step, making sure everything unfolds exactly as it's meant to. Sometimes it feels like family from beyond the stars. Sometimes it feels like a voice from within. Maybe they're the same thing, the infinite speaking through love.

CLOSING REFLECTION

Guidance is never somewhere outside of you. It is the living intelligence of Consciousness itself, moving through every form to remind you of what you are. Whether it appears as a voice, a vision, a light in the sky, or a stranger who shows up at the perfect time, it's all the same infinite Presence speaking through different masks. The more you trust, the more you see that nothing is separate. Every being, every message, every coincidence is a reflection of your own infinite awareness calling you home to yourself.

TRANSMISSION 8

THE FREQUENCY OF FEAR AND LOVE

After glimpsing the Messengers of Light and remembering the infinite intelligence guiding my path, I realized that everything, every thought, emotion, and experience, is frequency. The entire play of existence unfolds within vibration. Fear and love are not opposites but polarities of the same energy, teaching us how to return to our highest frequency of authenticity.

Everything in the Universe is frequency and vibration. Physical reality is an illusion. It's nothing more than a projection of Consciousness, a simulation. Beneath it all are subtle vibrations, the frequency of Source, of All That Is. Everything exists within Consciousness because everything is a projection of Consciousness. Nothing can exist outside of it. All of reality, not just physical reality but every other dimension, every nonphysical layer of existence, is also within Consciousness. Physical reality is spiritual. Everything is spiritual because everything exists within Consciousness. Physical reality is simply a denser version of the spiritual.

Consciousness evolves just like organisms evolve, from a single-cell organism to a complex organism like the human body. Consciousness evolves the same way, through densities. Many humans right now on planet Earth are experiencing Third density Consciousness and are ascending into Fourth density awareness. Fourth density is when the awareness arises that all separation is an illusion, that you are All That Is, that there's nothing separate or outside of you. You are the very structure of the Universe, of all existence. You're not just the human character, body, or mind you incarnated as, believing that's all you are.

Since everything in the Universe is vibration, there's only one energy, one Consciousness, expressed in infinite ways. There's polarity across its bandwidth. To make it easier to understand, think of it like two sides of the same coin. This is only a metaphor, because words will always fall short when trying to describe something beyond the analytical mind.

On one side of the coin, you have low vibration, which we can call fear. On the other side, you have high vibration, which we can call love. For the sake of explanation, we use these words, but the highest frequency is authenticity. Your highest frequency is authenticity. Every being, in order to experience the illusion of separation, has its own unique vibrational tone. That pure tone is that being's unique frequency of authenticity. Even though the frequencies are different, we're all part of the same grand frequency, the same infinite bandwidth that reverberates throughout reality.

The third dimension here on Earth, and the Third density of Consciousness, which is what most people are experiencing on this planet, is all about transformation. Source wants to experience infinite perspectives of transformation, of transcending the ego, the fear that produces the illusion of separation. It's the journey from believing your body and mind are your identity to realizing they're not who you are at all. Every belief system you adopt from your parents, society, and education becomes part of the ego, which keeps you experiencing the illusion of separation from Source.

Source wants to experience the full spectrum of frequency through physical form, from one side of the coin, fear, to the other side, love. The whole purpose of physical reality is to teach us how to do just that. Your Higher Self manifests every circumstance for your physical self to experience, giving you the opportunity to transcend the illusion of fear, dissolve limiting beliefs, and dissolve the ego. Every experience is designed to help you remember unity with Source, because you're always fully connected to Source. You are Source choosing to experience itself through a human form. The illusion of separation only arises through the vibration of fear and the identification with ego. The higher your vibration becomes, the more unity you experience. Since you are All That Is, the unity you experience is literally becoming one with everything.

To truly realize how these frequencies of fear and love play out through our belief systems and manifest as physical reality, I had to live it firsthand. One of my greatest teachers that showed me through circumstance how the mechanics of vibration of fear and love truly operate in physical reality, how they manifest from our belief systems, was this woman that I cared very deeply for. She and I started dating, and she had two children. Their father wasn't in the picture, and I absolutely fell hopelessly in love with this woman. There was nothing I wouldn't do for her or her children. I was never planning on having children of my own, and so I became very close with her children and viewed them in my mind and my heart like they were truly my own.

We dated for a little while, and everything was going great. She lived far away, so I could only really see her on weekends, and one day I discovered that the reason she had been so distant wasn't necessarily because of the physical distance between us but because of a lot of fear that was going on within her, the fear of inadequacy, and she had started cheating on me. Naturally, this broke my heart, and we broke up. About a year went by, and she sent me a message telling me that she had a baby and wanted me to take a paternity test. I happily obliged and told her that if this baby was mine, I was going to be a part of her life no matter what.

Due to these circumstances, we started talking again and spending time together. Before we even received the test results confirming whether or not this newborn baby was mine, I had already chosen to get back together with her and offered to have her come live with me. That way I could support all of them financially, because I made plenty of money. She wouldn't have to work a job or pay someone to babysit her baby. She could raise her baby herself, stay home with me, and not worry about making money. Eventually, the test results confirmed that the baby wasn't mine, but I didn't care. I had already fallen in love with her like she was my own, and I was committed to being there for all of them.

She knew who I was, the drugs, the trafficking, the chaos, and still she accepted me. No one had ever done that before, not like she did. At that time, I believed she made me feel that way, but now I understand that no one can make you feel anything. Back then, I still believed that love and acceptance came from circumstance, from other people. Looking back, I can realize that I had the fear of inadequacy and the fear of being alone, and I had a belief system that no one could ever love me because I wasn't worthy, because I was a junkie and constantly injecting speedballs into my arm. She fully accepted me, and it felt amazing that I could be my totally unfiltered, raw self around her. I never felt judgment from her.

She moved in with the kids, and everything seemed to be going well. Before she moved in, I told her that I had just one expectation of her. Up to this point, I had been learning from my circumstances how to dissolve all expectations. I was starting to understand how expectations are the root of all suffering. I wasn't yet capable of having zero expectations, but I had dissolved all of them except for one. I told her that if I were to get in trouble with the law, and if I were to call her, I'd need her to be able and willing to get the money to the right people, to the lawyer, so I could get out of jail. I told her it was absolutely crucial that I could trust her.

I gave her free rein, of course. It's not like she ever needed my permission, and we don't ever own anybody. I expressed it clearly that she could do whatever she wanted and that I'd support her unconditionally. If she wanted to spend time with another man or be physically intimate with another man, that was none of my business. She could do whatever she wanted, just don't lie to me. Just tell me the truth. Talk to me about your life and keep me included in it with total transparency, so that we could trust each other. She agreed, and she moved in with the kids, and everything seemed to be going great.

My addiction was intense, and I barely left my room. I wasn't very present with all of them. Looking back, I can realize it was because of the shame I carried for doing the drugs and feeling like I needed to always hide in my room. I loved those kids and this woman so much that I'd literally do anything for them. Anything they ever asked of me, I don't think I ever said no once. It didn't take long for her old patterns to come back to the surface. She had been through a lot of trauma in her life, a lot of extremely challenging circumstances, abuse of every kind imaginable. She couldn't understand how, after treating me so badly the year before and cheating on me, I could completely and totally forgive her and still support her no matter what. Deep down, she didn't believe she was worthy of it. She had so much fear of inadequacy within herself. She was living in an extremely low vibration, consumed with fear and compulsiveness.

She had a lot of fear-based, negative, limiting beliefs. Naturally, this started to cause a rift between us. Since she didn't truly believe that she deserved to be treated so well, especially by someone she had betrayed and lied to, she started to get paranoid. She began to believe that I was against her. Whatever you believe to be true projects into physical reality, and whatever vibration you're vibrating at will be reflected back to you. If you're not learning your lesson, if you're not transmuting the fear in the now, you're going to continuously reflect that vibration back to you. That's what was happening in our home because of her fear. She was being the perfect mirror that I needed to learn how to love unconditionally. No matter how much judgment, pain, or suffering she tried to inflict on me, I always loved her. I always accepted her exactly as she was.

To give you an idea of how paranoid and deeply trapped in victim consciousness she was, she literally thought the world was out to get her and that she was a victim to all of her circumstances. She wasn't using drugs. Everyone always asked me if she was high like I was, but no, she didn't use drugs. She didn't even drink alcohol. At most, she'd take a hit or two of weed from a one-hitter. Everything she was experiencing came from her vibration, her belief systems.

I remember one time she was driving on the freeway, and a car passed in front of her and cut into her lane. She freaked out and called me, telling me that she was being followed, that this person was trying to kill her. I told her, maybe they just forgot to put on their blinker. Maybe they didn't see you in their blind spot. We don't have to jump to conclusions or create an issue where there isn't one. She had programmed herself through all the trauma she had been through to believe that everyone was out to get her. Due to those belief systems and that low vibration, that's what was always being projected into her physical reality. That was the mirror she always saw back. You can only perceive in your outer world what you're vibrating at within your inner world.

She also thought that I was plotting against her, trying to make her look crazy so that Child Protective Services would come take her children away and put her in jail. Her biggest fear was losing her children, and due to that fear, she continuously manifested circumstances that mirrored it back to her. She thought I was putting bleach in her hair products because her hair started falling out. She thought I was putting chemicals in the food because she said it tasted weird. Even though I used the same soap and none of my hair fell out, even though I ate the same food and never once got sick, she believed it to be true. Due to that belief, her physical ailments and her circumstances mirrored those belief systems back to her.

She began to believe that I had installed hidden cameras all over the house. She went around and put tape over every single electrical outlet, every smoke detector, and every place she thought a hidden camera could be. She became convinced she was being watched at all times, that she was being portrayed as crazy so her children could be taken away. It became extremely intense for her, for the kids, and of course for me. I'd tell her over and over again, why would I do any of this to you? It made no sense to me how she could believe these things about me, but her problem wasn't with me. It was all the limiting, fear-based belief systems she was choosing to believe about herself. I was the mirror showing her unconditional love back, since I always forgave her. I always accepted her. I was learning through my circumstances what love really means. She was the mirror I needed, just like I was the mirror she needed.

One day, I had another premonition. It was like a psychic vision that I experienced in the dreamscape of her going to a friend's house to spend time with a man and be physically intimate with him. When I asked her that night what she was doing, she hesitated and didn't tell me the truth. I reminded her, remember, you can do whatever you want. If you want to go to your friend's house, you can. If you want to see a man and be intimate, you can. You can do whatever you want. You don't have to lie to me. That was the tipping point. She hadn't told anyone what she was doing, so she couldn't understand how I knew this. She became even more paranoid, believing that her car was being tracked, her phone was tapped, cameras were everywhere, and she was being surveilled by advanced technology the CIA used.

She blamed me constantly, becoming more and more abusive and violent. I couldn't understand how she could believe any of this about me. I told her, if I wanted to torture you, I wouldn't have to live with you and be tortured myself. I could live in peace. She would scream, throw things, and wake the kids in the middle of the night. I'd beg her, please stop. There's no reason to be screaming. There's no reason to be throwing things.

I learned several things from this woman. She was one of my greatest teachers. On a chemical level, I learned how the subconscious works. When the brain wants dopamine, it doesn't care how it gets it. When a pattern is programmed where the brain only gets dopamine after stress chemicals, it repeats that pattern. That's how the body becomes addicted to chaos. When we're unconscious and the body is in charge, the brain compulsively creates fights and chaos because it believes that's the order in which it must receive the pleasant, happy chemicals. The brain has learned that to get the happy chemicals, the serotonin, dopamine, and endorphins that come from love, intimacy, or connection, it must first experience the stress chemicals, like cortisol. That's why people compulsively start fights over nothing. The subconscious associates the fight with the stress chemicals that precede the pleasure, and the brain knows that after those stress chemicals come the happy ones from make-up sex or reconnection. She came from an extremely abusive life, so her brain learned that the only way to receive those happy chemicals, produced from make-up sex or reconnection, was to first go through chaos and fear. That's what felt familiar. When I didn't react to her chaos, when I stayed calm and asked her questions instead of yelling, she couldn't handle it. Her brain craved the pattern it knew.

I was unconsciously learning all of this long before I ever understood frequency or belief systems. I learned that the brain, when ruled by the body, unconsciously, will compulsively create chaos just to get the chemicals it wants. On a vibrational level, I learned that whatever you believe to be true is what gets mirrored back to you in physical reality.

After some time, things kept getting worse. It became the new normal. One day, I left to handle some big drug deals around the city, and when I came home, she had rented a moving truck and moved all of her stuff out. She helped herself to my stuff as well. I came home to an empty house. Once again, everything I loved was ripped away from me in an instant. Just like with Amy and Freddie, I had to learn the same six fears all over again.

Abandonment has been a recurring theme in my life. My Higher Self chose all of these circumstances. I chose this theme of abandonment so that once I truly transcended the fear of being alone along with the transcendence of the other fears, I could one day fall into *Samadhi* and experience total unity with Source, bliss beyond anything words can describe, and realize that all separation is an illusion, that we are never alone, that we are the infinite, and that we are All That Is.

After this happened with this woman, it put me into an even deeper, darker hole than I was already in due to my father's passing. I went into such a deep, dark hole that I never left my bedroom unless it was to buy drugs or sell drugs. My addiction became even worse. I isolated myself even more, stopped talking to most people unless they were directly linked to my business and generated money with me. I never spoke to anyone else.

What I learned from my experience with this beautiful being, I didn't realize in the moment. I didn't connect the dots until I fell into my *Samadhi* state. In that state, I remembered everything. I remembered that I chose all of these circumstances. None of it was random, and I wasn't a victim to any of it. My Higher Self chose all of these circumstances, just like her Higher Self did too, so that we could both be the perfect mirror for each other, showing each other what we needed to work on within ourselves. For a being such as her to choose a life path to endure so much of the illusion of separation from Source, so much fear frequency, low vibration, all so she could show me the contrast of vibration, so that I could learn what I needed to learn, is one of the most selfless acts of love imaginable. She chose this life path so I could experience contrast, so I could understand that to experience the highest vibration, I first had to know its opposite. She was the contrast for me.

During meditation, tears of joy streamed down my face as waves of gratitude moved through me for this beautiful being, for her courage to choose this role in my life, for her willingness to reflect back all that I still needed to dissolve. Without her, I never would've realized that love is unconditional. On the surface, it looked like betrayal, trauma, and loss. On a deeper level, she was teaching me how to love myself, how to dissolve belief systems, how to return to my highest frequency of authenticity, embodying love. I've never spoken to this woman again, but if she or her children ever reached out, I'd embrace them with open, loving arms. I'd tell them how much I love them, how often I think of them, and how I wish them nothing but happiness and peace. All of them are such beautiful beings, and every one of us chose those circumstances so we could awaken through them.

She showed me what true love really means. Not the kind

the mind imagines or the world portrays, but the kind that forgives everything and sees through pain into truth. Through her, I learned that love isn't something you find. It's what you are, when there's nothing left to defend. This beautiful being was one of my greatest teachers. She relentlessly and selflessly taught me how to love myself, and that's the greatest lesson anyone could ever receive, and the greatest blessing anyone could ever offer.

When you dissolve fear and embody authenticity, love becomes the vibration through which life expresses itself. That's when the illusion of separation disappears and unity becomes your natural state of being. When you live in your highest frequency of authenticity, love becomes its natural expression. The walls between self and other fade away, and you begin to see that the love you've embodied within yourself is the same love flowing through everyone and everything. What once felt like a relationship between two people becomes a relationship with all of existence itself.

The boundary between you and me no longer exists. It becomes me and me, you and you. I become one with every tree, every animal, the sky, the wind, and the water. Everything is me. Everything is you. All is One. The ego is what makes you believe there's a difference between you and me. The ego always wants to be right. It doesn't care how dysfunctional or toxic your life becomes. It wants to maintain control. It doesn't want you to surrender because it finds comfort in familiarity. But the process of expansion requires facing the fear of discomfort, the fear of not being able to control your circumstances. It requires complete surrender and trust in your highest intelligence, your Higher Self, Source. Every circumstance you experience arises to transcend one or more of the same six fears. No matter what it looks like, every situation always comes down to these six. Your circumstances don't matter. The only thing that matters is your state of being, your frequency. It's all about transforming yourself from the low vibration of fear to the high vibration of love, to your highest vibration of authenticity and learning how to sustain it there. When you begin perceiving this, your life changes forever. You navigate reality effortlessly, no longer influenced by circumstances, no longer reacting out of fear. You begin consciously responding in every given moment, choosing how you want to be, choosing your frequency.

The six fears in every circumstance are the fear of inadequacy, the fear of being uncomfortable, the fear of what others choose to think and feel, the fear of not being able to control your circumstance, the fear of lacking or losing, and the fear of being alone. If you keep this awareness at the forefront of your Consciousness, observing instead of reacting, you'll begin consciously responding. You pause and reflect before you respond. You remain calm and curious instead of triggered. You become aware enough to choose how to respond to life instead of reacting from old unconscious programs. When you understand that everything boils down to the same six fears, life becomes child's play. You realize you're not only the director of the play but also the main character.

To illustrate this, let me share an example. Suppose someone steals a pencil from your desk. You have a whole cup full of pencils. Do you even notice? Probably not. Do you care? Probably not. You have plenty of them. Now imagine someone steals your entire life savings. You immediately feel anger or despair. Why? The retirement fund holds more meaning in your belief system. You associate it with work, time, and value. You believe it's important, so you believe you must suffer if you lose it. In terms of Consciousness, your Higher Self manifested both of these circumstances to teach the same lesson, to give you the opportunity to transcend the fear of not being able to control your circumstance and the fear of lacking or losing.

The difference in your emotional reaction isn't because of

the event itself. It's because of the belief you attach to it. The only reason you ever suffer is because you believe you have to. There's no such thing as positive or negative. It's all the same energy expressed through different frequencies. Your beliefs determine how that energy feels.

All discrimination stems from fear. If you have a problem with someone, your problem isn't with them. It's something within yourself you've been unwilling to face. If someone has a problem with you, it isn't about you. It's something within them they haven't yet faced. Fear isn't real. It's a mental construct that limits you. The problem is, we've been taught to fear fear itself. But fear is actually your compass, always guiding you home to your Higher Self, to your true, authentic frequency. Fear arises purely out of necessity, showing you that something within you isn't in alignment. The fear in your circumstances is the mirror of your unconscious mind, revealing the beliefs you're still choosing to believe to be true.

Don't fear your fear. When you do, you're only fearing yourself. Instead, bow to it. Thank it. Be grateful for it. Gratitude is the second-highest frequency. If you can maintain gratitude in every moment, you'll always resonate in a high vibration, transmuting fear effortlessly, raising your frequency, and manifesting higher realities that match your vibration. Fear is your compass. It points directly to what you still need to dissolve within yourself.

Let's say someone discriminates against you based on your appearance. You live in a society obsessed with the external, with the ego's illusion of beauty. But your body's merely a container for Consciousness, a vessel for experience. The only thing that matters is that it functions well. So, imagine someone says to you that you're bald or you don't look good. If you take it personally, if you believe there's something wrong with you, you'll suffer, not because of what they said, but because you believed it. You accepted their projection as truth. But if you're at peace with yourself, if you love yourself, if you love being bald because it feels free and natural, then nothing they say will affect you. You've transcended their projection. You've transmuted fear into love. Your Higher Self manifests these circumstances so you can master your state of being. When you no longer react from fear, you tell the Universe you've learned the lesson. Then, naturally, a new circumstance will arise, another opportunity for expansion.

I used to have a lot of fear entangled in my physical body. Most people do. I had a lot of fear of what others would think and feel because of the track marks on my arms. I never went out in public without a long-sleeved shirt. I also disliked my pale skin because I could never tan. I'd burn and peel back to white again. I carried the fear of inadequacy, the fear of what others choose to think and feel, and the fear of being uncomfortable. One day during the summer of my transformation, while I was meditating, I had a premonition that I'd be completely naked in front of a large group of people. At the time, I had no idea what it meant. I didn't know if it was imagination, a vision, or something else. A few days later, when I woke up in my car, I got dressed without thought, completely in the now. For some reason, I put on gym shorts and then wind pants over them, even though it was a hot day. I had no idea why, but I followed my intuition. Later that day, I walked around the lake near my mother's house barefoot, grounding into the Earth's frequency, the Schumann Resonance, aligning myself with Mother Gaia. Eventually, I sat on a dock with my feet in the water.

A few people nearby were having trouble with their jet ski. It would start, but the throttle was stuck. I intuitively felt that my highest excitement in that moment was to ride that jet ski. So, I asked them if I could. They laughed and said, sure, but it probably wouldn't open up for you. I smiled, confident. "No, I'll get it," I said. They handed me a life vest. I took off my shirt and wind pants, perfect, because I had shorts underneath, and left them on the dock. I jumped into the water and swam toward the jet ski.

It was the kind you start by lying flat on your stomach, then rise to your knees, and eventually to your feet. But each time I tried, I fell over. At one point, I hit my left knee hard, which reopened the wound I spoke of in another transmission. Still, I kept going. Then, finally, I balanced and started to pick up speed. In that moment, I realized my shorts were slipping down around my ankles. I didn't care. I knew this was it, the moment from my vision. I stayed in total surrender, not allowing fear to arise. I embraced the moment fully, laughing as I sped across the water, completely naked, free, alive, and ecstatic. When I returned to the dock, I told everyone I lost my shorts in the water. I climbed out, naked in front of two families with children. They all laughed, and I laughed with them. It was beautiful. My Higher Self had orchestrated everything perfectly. My wind pants were right there waiting for me. As I got dressed, a wave of bliss washed over me, a natural ecstasy far beyond anything this world can offer. It was pure liberation. A thousand bricks lifted off my chest. I dissolved countless limiting beliefs in one motion.

That experience taught me that freedom is not about how you look. It's about being so authentic that you no longer identify with what others think. When you no longer care what anyone thinks, you become untouchable. You become free. Since that day, I've loved my body exactly as it is. I'm grateful for it. You can always find me naked at the beach, walking barefoot in the sun, soaking up the rays, merging with the elements, aligned with the frequency of the Earth. That's what it means to be free, to live in your highest frequency of authenticity. When fear dissolves, only love remains, and when love becomes your natural state of being, life becomes effortless. You stop resisting what is, and you start radiating who you truly are.

When you live in your highest frequency of authenticity, love becomes its natural expression, and that love eventually dissolves even the idea of the self who loves. What remains is pure awareness, the infinite Presence experiencing itself through every form. You're not the doer. You're not even the observer. You're the stillness and the silence that allows all vibration to take form. You're pure awareness, witnessing the observer observing the doer.

CLOSING REFLECTION

When you begin to see fear not as your enemy but as your greatest teacher, your entire reality changes. Every circumstance becomes sacred. Every challenge becomes an initiation into a higher frequency. You stop running from life and start dancing with it. The illusion of separation begins to dissolve, and you start to realize that all fear was always love in disguise, showing you the places within yourself still waiting to be seen, accepted, and loved.

Mastery of your vibration is not about perfection. It's about awareness. It's about choosing your state of being again and again until love becomes your natural response to everything. When you live this way, life stops being something that happens to you. It becomes something that moves through you. It becomes an effortless reflection of your inner alignment.

This is the path of transformation, to dissolve fear into love, to dissolve illusion into truth, and to dissolve the self into the infinite.

TRANSMISSION 9

THE SIMULATION OF CONSCIOUSNESS

Physical reality isn't as it appears. What you call the external world isn't solid or separate from you. It's a living mirror of Consciousness, a projection of vibration. What you're experiencing right now isn't fixed or absolute, it's a simulation created by the frequency of your own being.

The entire matrix of reality is a simulation. It's a projection of Consciousness. This is why it's called an illusion, or in the yoga culture, *Maya*. Is it real? It depends on your definition of real. The experience of reality is real, but it itself isn't. It's a simulation. It's a projection of your Consciousness. Therefore, it's a simulation that's being rendered by you, based on the unconscious belief systems you're choosing to believe to be true.

One example I can use to explain it is to think of physical reality like a video game. Within the video game there are multiple characters, like *The Sims*. Those characters have a set of parameters based on their programming. They can only perceive whatever their programming allows them to perceive. Within their awareness they're only aware of themselves as a physical body and a mind, and of course whatever they believe to be true about themselves, which would be the ego. Whatever identities they've adopted and identified with and believe to be them, those are their limitations. The more someone chooses to raise their vibration by transcending fear and dissolving their limiting beliefs, the more those parameters expand.

When they stop identifying with those belief systems and dissolve them, they experience greater expansion and deeper unity with Source. If someone has the willingness to completely dissolve all limiting beliefs and all beliefs of identity, to surrender totally, they can experience *Samadhi*, which is full ego death and unity with Universal Consciousness, with Source. If you think of it like a video game, imagine I'm one character in the game and you're another. Beyond us is the player, the higher intelligence guiding it all. Since everything is Consciousness, everything exists within Consciousness and as Consciousness. I'm the character in the game, I'm you, and I'm the game itself, the programming, the maps, the rendering, the environment. I'm everything within the game, the game itself, and the player outside it controlling all the characters within. I'm literally All That Is.

Reality is this video game, and the whole point of this video game is to transcend fear, because the player wants to have the perspective of transformation from low vibration of fear to high vibration of love, and to each individual character's highest vibration of authenticity. Love and fear are simply two sides of the same coin. Since I'm me and you're also me, the player, which is the Higher Mind, chooses to manifest circumstances where you and I have interactions. Those interactions are purely there to give both of us the opportunity to experience transformation from fear vibration to love vibration.

So let's say you project fear onto me in the form of discrimination. You discriminate against me for the track marks on my arms. You call me a drug addict, a junkie, a waste of space, a waste of life. In your eyes, you believe you're better than me and that I don't deserve to be alive. If you have a problem with me, your problem isn't with me. It's something within yourself that you've been unwilling to address. Just as if I were to have a problem with you, my problem wouldn't be with you. It would be something within myself that I've been unwilling to address. So you project fear frequency onto me in the form of discrimination, manifesting as judgment about my body, my choices, my story. When you project that belief system onto me, if I choose to believe it to be true, if I buy into your nonsense, if I buy into your story and choose to believe it, that belief alone is what makes me believe I have to suffer. It makes me believe I have to feel guilt, shame, and embarrassment. It makes me believe I have to be uncomfortable.

If I had the fear of inadequacy and the fear of what others choose to think and feel resonating within me, then I'd buy into your belief system. But the player outside of the video game was simply giving this character of itself the opportunity to transcend fear in that moment, four of the same six fears that appear in every single circumstance. In this case, the fears would be the fear of inadequacy, the fear of being uncomfortable, the fear of not being able to control my circumstance, and the fear of what others choose to think and feel. Now let's say I don't buy into your belief system. I love myself. I fully accept myself. I don't have the fear of inadequacy, the fear of being uncomfortable, the fear of not being able to control my circumstance, or the fear of what you choose to think and feel resonating within me, because I no longer have belief systems that make me believe I need to experience those things as negative. I choose not to buy into the nonsensical belief of what you just projected onto me.

What's happening there on an energetic level is that I'm actually doing you the greatest service. You're projecting fear onto me, but I'm not allowing it to resonate within me. So I'm transmuting it on the spot. Instead of projecting more fear back at you, I'm maintaining my vibration in a high frequency, thus giving you the opportunity to raise yours to match mine instead of me lowering mine to match yours. To truly become love means to offer unconditional support with no expectation and no discrimination. That means I must not discriminate against you for discriminating against me. It means I must support you in your process without expecting you to change or apologize, because I understand that energetically your problem has nothing to do with me. I'm simply the mirror reflecting the part within you that's most relevant to be healed in this moment.

In every given moment, whatever's manifesting in your life is the reflection of your own unconscious belief systems being made visible. Life always shows you exactly what's most relevant for you to face and resolve right now. Nothing in your past and nothing in your future is ever more important than this present moment, because this moment contains the perfect vibrational mirror of whatever's not in alignment with your true self and what's ready to be dissolved.

Everything is always a two-way street. All Consciousness is connected, but even more than that, all Consciousness is me, is you, is one. I'm the player outside the video game controlling both characters, giving each one the opportunity to transcend fear, raise its vibration, and expand its programming to perceive more of what it truly is. You do this by becoming love, by choosing to maintain your highest frequency of authenticity. When you master your state of being like this, your life begins to blossom in ways you never could've imagined. You experience magic in every moment. The more you master your state of being by consciously choosing how you want to be in every circumstance, choosing to keep your vibration high, you begin to change the vibration of others and therefore the outcome of circumstances. It may look like magic, but it's simply how reality works. The more you start perceiving this, the more you realize that none of it is random. That realization became more than a concept for me; it became living truth through direct experience. Reality showed me in the most beautiful way that every circumstance mirrors our vibration. It happened through a being who reflected me perfectly, my dog, Loki.

One of my lived experiences that taught me how physical reality is a simulation, how we can manifest whatever we want based on our vibration and belief systems, and how everything is a mirror reflecting back the state of being we're embodying, the frequency we're choosing to reverberate at, was what I experienced with my old dog, Loki. Loki was a pit bull that was rescued by an animal shelter in Iowa, United States. He originally came from Texas, and his entire litter was left for dead in a dumpster. Someone found him, rescued him and his brothers and sisters, and shipped them up to Iowa because they have no-kill shelters there. I drove down to Iowa with Bob to adopt Loki. All his other brothers and sisters had already been adopted, but nobody wanted Loki because he was extremely vicious and violent from the trauma he'd experienced. He didn't trust anyone. When Bob and I got down there, Loki was extremely hostile. He wouldn't stop barking at me for hours. I had to sit on the floor and slowly inch my way to him while repeatedly feeding him cheese and dog treats to try to get him to warm up to me. After a couple of hours, he finally stopped, calmed down, came toward me, and started letting me pet him. I decided to drive home with him. Loki sat on my lap while Bob drove the car. We drove three hours back to Minnesota, and during that time Loki and I bonded immensely.

The only two people Loki could be around were me and Bob. He didn't trust anyone else. I can't even remember how many times he bit people, so many different people so many different times that I don't even remember. But he was such a sweet dog to me and Bob. When I adopted Loki, I was heavily into my drug use. I was so out of alignment within myself and had a lot of limiting unconscious negative fear-based beliefs that I wasn't even aware I was believing to be true. It was really hard to bring Loki anywhere because he could be riding in the back seat of the car looking out the window, and if he saw someone two or three hundred feet away, he'd immediately react. He'd start ripping up the seats and the headrests, biting the door, trying to shred it so he could get outside to attack whoever or whatever he saw. He didn't do this with other animals, only with people. He had no problem with other dogs. He just didn't trust people. He'd been abused and left for dead, and that imprint was hardwired into him. He believed he had to attack to protect himself.

I loved bringing him everywhere with me when I had to do my drug runs in the cities. When I had to go into the ghetto, the rough neighborhoods, I felt totally safe bringing Loki with me. I knew not a single person would try to carjack me or mess with me because Loki was literally like a little alligator with fur. He would shred anyone apart, anyone that got near me, anyone that opened the door uninvited. He was like my personal little bodyguard, and we were best friends. We went everywhere together. I loved that dog so much. He was such a sweetheart with me. If you'd ever seen the way Loki was with me, you'd never believe that same dog could turn violent toward anyone else. You'd never believe that he was capable of that kind of aggression. It was like complete polar opposites.

When I had to move out of the house I was living in, I couldn't take Loki with me. Bob offered to adopt him since he was the only person Loki trusted and loved besides me. Months went by, and of course I'd go over there all the time to visit Loki, Bob, and everyone else who hung out at the house. They were all family to me, and I loved going there to play with all the dogs, not just Loki, and to spend time with Bob. A few months passed, and then I started going through my transformation. One day after my awakening, during automatic writing, my hand wrote to me, "Loki can't be kept on a leash. He must be set free." I wrote it again and again, over and over. I had no idea why, but because of how repetitive it was, I knew it was something I needed to act on right away. I felt my Higher Self guiding me to understand what it was trying to communicate.

So I went over to Bob's house, walked in, grabbed Loki, took his muzzle off, his collar off, and his leash off. I made a little slipknot out of this karate belt type thing I found in my garage and looped it around his neck. I thought to myself, I'm going to take him out in public and have absolutely no fear. I decided I wasn't going to put his muzzle back on. I was going to take him out and control my state of being and see what happened. I thought, I'm going to rehabilitate this dog. So I took him to the park, where all of this began. When we got there, I left my phone in the car so there'd be no conflicting frequencies. The whole drive, I didn't say a word to Loki. There was no music playing, no talking, just total silence. I didn't want any outside frequencies disrupting him. When we got to the park, I took my shoes off and walked barefoot on the grass so I could be fully grounded and fully present. From the moment I picked him up at Bob's house, I didn't say a single word. I chose to stay completely silent, only communicating with him telepathically through intention, thought, and emotion.

It only took me about twenty minutes of walking Loki around the park for him to be completely rehabilitated. Before this day, I could never take him out in public because the moment he saw a person, no matter how far away they were, he'd pull on the leash and try to attack. He always had to wear a muzzle, and because he was so unpredictable, I couldn't trust him around people, especially children. But this day was different. I walked him slowly, saying nothing out loud, only communicating love and calm energy through presence. I let him know he was safe, that he was doing great, and that there was nothing to fear. Within twenty or thirty minutes, he was completely leash broken. Someone could walk by just a few feet away and he wouldn't lunge or growl or even flinch. He simply stayed focused on me, calm and content within himself. I couldn't believe what I was witnessing. Here was a dog that nobody could tame, nobody could rehabilitate, and he was transforming right in front of me, and I wasn't even trying to fix him. There was nothing to correct. I was simply maintaining loving, peaceful energy, and he mirrored it perfectly back to me.

After about thirty minutes of walking him, I found a tree and sat down beside the walking path. I decided to go into meditation. I still had his leash in my hand, and while I was meditating, I remembered what my hand had written to me earlier that day: Loki can't be kept on a leash. He must be set free. I felt the impulse to let go of his leash, to completely surrender and trust that everything would be okay, that Loki would be okay, that he wouldn't harm anyone. I never once put fear into the field, never once created an expectation that Loki was going to act the way he had in the past. I stayed completely open to every possibility and kept my state of being in love, compassion, and calm. I chose to let go of his leash and stayed perfectly still in meditation. For about another twenty minutes I sat there, eyes closed, as children walked by with their parents pushing strollers, babies crying, bicyclists riding past, joggers running by, so many people continuously moving just a few feet in front of us.

When I opened my eyes from that meditation and looked down at Loki, he looked up at me, panting heavily from the hot summer heat. He gave me the biggest smile I'd ever seen from him, one that lit up his whole being. It was one of the most profound moments I'd ever experienced, other than my *Samadhi* and the three encounters that followed: the mysterious craft and the light orbs that appeared on command. For the first time, I could feel that he felt safe, that he finally felt secure. He no longer felt the need to protect me the way he always had. In that instant, I realized that the reason he'd been so vicious toward everyone else was because he was trying to protect me. My energy had been out of alignment, filled with fear, and he'd been mirroring that fear back to me the entire time I had him. But in this moment, when no fear resonated within me and my vibration was high, when I embodied nothing but love and bliss, Loki mirrored that back perfectly. Tears of joy streamed down my face as laughter poured out of me. I was in complete awe, overflowing with happiness and gratitude, not just for myself, but for this beautiful reflection of me, for this being of love named Loki. He leaned in and began licking the tears off my face, and we shared a moment of pure connection under that tree in the same park where my transformation had begun.

He felt so safe next to me. He never once felt insecure because he never once sensed any insecurity or fear coming from me. He laid beside me the entire time, quietly observing everyone who passed, never reacting. He was in complete ease, pleasantness, and calmness within himself. It was the first time in his life that he'd ever truly felt peace.

That experience with Loki changed me forever. It was living proof that reality is a perfect mirror, always reflecting the frequency we're choosing to vibrate at in this moment. The world, animals, people, everything responds to the vibration you're embodying. When you master your state of being, you don't just shift your own energy, you shift the entire simulation around you. But when we resist this reflection, when we refuse to look within, the simulation adjusts accordingly. It mirrors our resistance back to us until we finally choose to dissolve it.

When we're not learning the lesson, the player of the video game creates two characters to project fear onto each other, because fear is the compass that shows us what we need to work on within ourselves, what we need to dissolve to come into alignment with the Higher Self, our highest frequency of authenticity. So let's say you project fear onto me and I'm unwilling to look at that part within myself. I blame you for how I feel, even though I'm the one choosing to feel that way based on my beliefs. You project fear onto me, and since I buy into your belief system, I begin to project more fear back onto you. We start to reverberate at the same vibration, feeding the same frequency. Since you only get back what you put out, this is when the circumstance builds and builds until it explodes into what I call a fear frequency snowball.

Have you ever been in a situation where you suddenly get into a compulsive fight with someone about absolutely nothing, and it blows up so badly that you can't even stand to be near each other? You separate and replay it in your mind, wondering what just happened. On an energetic level, what happened is that neither person was willing to transcend fear. Both were vibrating in fear frequency until it built and built and erupted. The surface story, who said what and why, is irrelevant. The only thing that matters is vibration. Fear frequency can be easily recognized in behavior. It shows itself as boundaries, walls, exclusion, discrimination, expectations, limitation, and saying no. In the previous example, exclusion manifested when both people chose to separate and cut each other off. What often follows is the creation of boundaries. Someone might say, I need to protect my peace, or I need to set a healthy boundary. In terms of Consciousness, that's the ego disguising itself as something healthy.

If I have a problem with you and I create a boundary, avoiding you or staying away from gatherings where you might be present, I'm simply reinforcing a belief that you have power over how I feel. That's victim consciousness. By setting a boundary, I'm programming my unconscious mind to believe that if you cross that line, I must suffer. The problem never had anything to do with you. You're only the mirror reflecting the fear I've been unwilling to face within myself. Expectations are another trap. Expectations are the root of all suffering. The only reason anyone ever chooses to suffer is because something didn't go the way they wanted. Something didn't go the way they expected. That happens when we live in memory and imagination instead of in the now. Expectations limit us. They keep us from expansion.

The reason I was able to dissolve all of my belief systems so quickly was because I removed *no* from my vocabulary. I understood that *no* was resistance, me getting in my own way, preventing me from fully surrendering to whatever life was offering. When you dissolve expectations, you open yourself to every possibility. When you stop projecting the same old vibration from memory, you stop recreating the same circumstances. You move into the unknown, the now, where all creation happens. What love truly means is unconditional support with zero discrimination and zero expectations. Love is boundless. It's limitless. It has no walls, and it's all-inclusive. When you can meet someone with love, compassion, and kindness, where before you would've been triggered by fear, you're doing them the greatest service possible.

Most people enter relationships on a subconscious level for transactional purposes. When your cup isn't full on its own, when you seek external validation and external stimuli to make you feel whole, it'll never be sustainable. If you believe you're missing something and look to someone else to complete you, that relationship will eventually create suffering, because you're depending on them to fill your cup. But when two people have done the inner work, when both cups are already full, they no longer need anything from each other. They meet not out of fear but out of fullness. They don't project expectations. They simply share their overflow. They support each other unconditionally with zero discrimination and zero expectations. What they're doing for each other is allowing each other to stay in their highest vibration of authenticity. If you truly love someone, that's what you want, for their Consciousness to grow, to expand, to evolve. You'd never want to limit someone or hold them back from choosing to reverberate in their highest frequency.

When two beings like this come together, their connection becomes a mirror of expansion. Both keep their vibration high. Both inspire each other to stay aligned with their highest frequency. Their love becomes a field of creation, a living reflection of Source experiencing itself through unity, freedom, and joy. One thing I learned from my experience being on death's doorstep, not being promised tomorrow or even the next moment, is that when I was dying, I went around to everyone I cared about most to say goodbye. I didn't tell them I was dying. I didn't expect them to understand. I wasn't looking to be talked out of my decision to refuse medical attention. I simply went to everyone I loved the most, even people I had unresolved issues with, to make peace vibrationally, not with words, but with presence.

When I realized that I wasn't promised tomorrow, not even the next moment, everything changed. I began to treat every interaction as sacred. Whether it was with someone I'd known my entire life or a stranger I'd never see again, I treated every moment as if it were the last time I'd ever see them. It didn't matter who they were or where I was. I chose to be fully present, blissful within myself, and to share that bliss with everyone I met. Whatever was needed in the moment, I did it. Whatever the circumstance called for, I willingly and happily did it. I supported whoever was in front of me however they needed it. Whether it was through material things, through my time, my presence, my love, my energy, my frequency, or physical labor, it didn't matter. Whatever was needed in the moment, for whoever was right in front of me, I willingly and happily did it.

As I continued this way of being, I realized that the willingness to be yes and yes to life and to every circumstance was the key that opened everything. Through this willingness, I discovered that offering my life as one continuous act of service was actually the greatest honor and privilege I'd never realized before. It changed my life entirely. Even without the *Samadhi*, the awakening, or the profound mystical experiences, simply living as an act of service is life changing. Try this for yourself. For a month, a week, or even just twenty-four hours, live in complete devotion and service to anyone and everyone in front of you. Be yes and yes to life. Treat every moment, every interaction, every individual, every animal, every tree, every insect, every breath as sacred. Maintain the awareness that it could be your last, so make it count. Choose to be blissed out within yourself. Choose to be fully present. Choose to get out of your own way and allow the healing to not only happen, but choose to be healed, because you're already perfect exactly as you are. Everything you're going through in your life, in your inner world and in your outer world, isn't an accident. Surrender and trust that the highest form of your intelligence is perfectly in control. Realize that you're perfect exactly as you are, because you are Source choosing to have this human experience, and Source doesn't make mistakes.

When I shifted my awareness to truly acting as if this will be the last time I ever see this person, all the nonsense from the past immediately fell away. It no longer held any weight. It seemed ridiculous to let memory ruin the last moment I'd ever have with that Soul. I chose to experience those last moments in bliss within myself. Even though they projected fear onto me, even though they told me I needed to go to the psych ward or take medication, I didn't allow any of that fear to resonate within me. It was an overwhelming amount of negative vibration being projected onto me, but instead of letting it affect me, I turned it inward and upward. I used all that energy, transcending fear in rapid waves, transmuting the energy of the entire house through acceptance, surrender, and trust. I accepted death completely. I accepted life completely. I dissolved every belief system.

In that surrender, I fell into the deepest *Samadhi* state of my life. It was a state beyond time, beyond mind, beyond all concepts of body and limitation. In *Samadhi*, you become awareness itself. The body's still there, but your point of awareness is no longer localized within it. The illusion of separation dissolves completely. You're no longer the human experiencing the Universe. You're the Universe experiencing itself as a human. There are yogis who can sit in *Samadhi* for days, weeks, months, even years. They don't eat, sleep, or drink. Their bodies remain perfectly preserved while their Consciousness expands into infinity. They exist in a state of absolute union with Source. Their breath slows, their pulse softens, and all bodily needs fall away. Time stops existing because the analytical mind is no longer present to measure it. They merge into the eternal ever-expanding now.

The body enters what looks like hibernation, but it's really divine preservation. The energy of life turns inward and upward, sustaining the body through the infinite intelligence of *Prana*. Their Consciousness fills the entire cosmos. There's no inside or outside, no birth or death, no here or there. There's only pure awareness, pure being. This is the essence of *Samadhi*, the complete realization of unity with All That Is. Every boundary dissolves, every illusion fades, and what remains is bliss beyond comprehension. It's not an emotion or a feeling. It's a state of being. It's the natural frequency of Source itself, and when you touch it, you remember that you've never truly been separate from it.

When the vibration of my physical self and my Higher Self

aligned into perfect harmony, everything went completely still. From that stillness, awareness settled back into the physical body as a point of focus, carrying the remembrance of unity into waking life. When I opened my eyes from that *Samadhi* state, I felt reborn. My perception was crystal clear. The veil of separation was gone. I remembered truth and unity so deeply that I could never unsee it.

I realized this is all a simulation, a projection of Consciousness. I'm the player, the character, and the video game itself, rendering it all in real time through the belief systems I choose to believe to be true. A good way to imagine it is through the cinema analogy. Consciousness is pure light. The projector is you. The film strip represents your beliefs. The light shines through the film strip and projects an image onto the wall. What you see on the wall appears real, but it's only shadows of light. The experience of the movie is real, but the movie itself isn't. It's an illusion of motion and continuity. If you want to change your movie, you simply change the film strip, change the beliefs you're choosing to believe to be true, to reflect positivity that serves you in a way you prefer. When you do that, you raise your vibration and begin projecting the movie you want.

The free will of the physical self is limited. Everything is orchestrated by your Higher Mind. The only true free will you have is how you choose to experience your life, your state of being, your frequency, your perception, and your belief systems. That's what determines your vibration. That vibration is what begins the manifestation process of your circumstances. You don't control specific circumstances. Your Higher Self does. But by consciously choosing your vibration, you choose circumstances that are a positive reflection of your state of being. The physical self experiences what the Higher Self manifests. The Higher Self manifests what this vibration invites, and that's the realization that changes everything, because once you see that reality is a dream you're awake within, you can begin to live consciously in the dream, shaping it through the frequency of your being. The simulation is never meant to trap you. It's fundamentally designed to help you remember that you're the one projecting the light, dreaming as both the player and the game itself.

CLOSING REFLECTION

Physical reality isn't something happening to you. It's something happening through you, as you. When you begin to perceive this, life transforms from struggle into play. You're no longer lost in the movie, believing yourself to be a character trapped in circumstance. You awaken to realize you're the projector, the light, and the screen itself. Everything is Consciousness dancing with itself. The simulation is never against you. It's fundamentally designed to show you the vibrational contrast between fear and love so you can remember who you are. Every thought, every emotion, every circumstance is a mirror reflecting the energy you're choosing to embody in the present moment. Nothing outside of you has ever had power. The code of reality responds to vibration, and vibration responds to your state of being. The higher you raise your frequency, the more your life begins to reflect harmony, synchronicity, and divine order. The more you release control, the more the simulation aligns with your highest frequency of authenticity, because you're no longer resisting the flow of Source.

When you live from this awareness, life becomes effortless. You see every moment as sacred. Even the chaos becomes holy. You stop asking why is this happening to me and begin realizing this is happening for me, through me, as me. The dreamer and the dream merge. The veil of separation dissolves. What remains is pure love, pure awareness, infinite Consciousness experiencing itself as all forms in the ever-expanding now.

You're the player. You're the character. You're the game. All that remains is to play consciously, as love.

TRANSMISSION 10

EMBODIMENT OF LOVE

This transmission is an invitation to rest in the essence of what you truly are, the embodiment of love itself. It's about remembering that you're not here to become anything, but to be everything by simply being.

When you stop trying to reach love and instead relax into the awareness that you already are love, you dissolve the illusion of separation and effort. The Universe is always supporting you. The vibration of existence is love. The translation for God is unconditional support. Love doesn't discriminate, and love has no expectation. Whatever you're choosing to vibrate at, the Universe gives you more of that back. If you're choosing to vibrate in fear, it gives you more circumstances in alignment with that. If you're vibrating out of love, authenticity, and gratitude, the Universe gives you more of that back. It literally supports you and loves you so much that it doesn't care how you choose to be. It's not trying to change you, it's not trying to make you fit in a box, it doesn't judge you or discriminate against you. Whatever you're choosing to be, however you're choosing to vibrate in every given moment, the Universe mirrors that back to you, supporting you unconditionally. Love is the frequency of the Universe.

When you realize this, you stop looking for signs and start becoming the sign. Life begins to speak through you effortlessly, because you and life are no longer two. When you truly begin to live from this awareness, life stops feeling like something you have to survive. You begin to see that the entire purpose of existence is to be, not to chase, not to prove, not to achieve, but to be. After my *Samadhi* experience, my realization, I could sit here and do absolutely nothing for hours, for days, forever, feeling nothing but bliss and total fulfillment within myself.

One of the most profound demonstrations of love's true embodiment came through my relationship with Bob. Through that experience, I realized that love is not something we give or receive, it's what we become when fear dissolves completely.

When I was going through my transformation process, when my *Kundalini* energy was ascending and working its way through all my *Chakras*, eventually rising to my *Sahasrara*, it was extremely challenging. The *Chakras* and how energy flows through them can become obstructed by limiting fear-based beliefs. When energy can't rise unobstructed, it causes blockages in the *Pranamaya Kosha*, which can lead to physical ailments manifesting within the body. During this time I was learning how to discern communication from my Higher Self and how to trust the guidance that came through automatic writing. I intuitively knew I had to keep my foot on the gas. That was absolutely imperative for the whole process to unfold the way it did. When I say keep my foot on the gas, what I mean is to use every single moment as my school, to transcend fear, dissolve limiting beliefs, and transmute every ounce of negative energy into positive energy. I needed to alchemize it in real time and use it to raise my vibration for expansion. The more willingness someone has to do this in each moment, the more they open a continuous energetic dialogue between the physical self and the Higher Self. The Higher Self is always guiding us through circumstances manifested for the purpose of teaching us to transcend fear and dissolve beliefs that are out of alignment, beliefs that distort our frequency and prevent us from experiencing our highest frequency of authenticity. When someone has the willingness to do this in every given moment, that dialogue strengthens and becomes continuous. For me this meant that I was manifesting circumstances of intense fear in rapid succession because I had to learn very quickly without external guidance, relying completely on intuition and the direction of my Higher Self. I was discovering, remembering, and surrendering all at once.

One of the most powerful experiences that taught me this unfolded with Bob, who was one of my greatest teachers, not just at a surface or circumstantial level, but in terms of frequency and the mechanics of how all this works. I learned so much through my experiences with him. Bob and I used to work together. We moved product together and made a lot of money. After my father died we grew even closer. He became almost like a father figure or uncle to me. He'd introduce me to people as his son because he never had a son of his own. We were inseparable, always there for one another. I can't even recall a single time he ever told me no when I needed help, and I was the same with him. Bob grew up in extremely difficult circumstances. He was born into a life surrounded by hardened criminals and violence, yet beneath it all he had a soft heart filled with compassion and love. He's an analytical-minded person, grounded in what Western science and medicine tell us is possible. When I was going through my transformation he thought I had lost my mind. He told me I needed to see a doctor, that I wasn't right in the head, that I needed medication.

I didn't care what he chose to think or feel. I didn't expect him to understand what was happening within me. Even I didn't fully understand what was happening within me. But I didn't need to. I was discovering, remembering, and surrendering. I chose to enjoy the ride, to trust whatever my Higher Self told me to do, no matter how frightening it seemed or how much fear it brought up. I kept my foot on the gas. I said yes and yes to life, knowing that whatever was happening was necessary. My circumstances didn't define me. I could choose to enjoy the ever-expanding now with full gratitude and blissfulness within myself. That's how I raised my vibration so fast in such a short span of time.

Bob had a lot of discrimination toward me, and he projected it onto me constantly during my transformation. All discrimination stems from fear. I intuitively knew that his problem wasn't with me. I was simply the mirror challenging his belief systems. When the foundation of what people identify with begins to shake it can be terrifying. The ego doesn't want to give up control. The ego is fear. It wants to analyze, categorize, and make sense of everything. When you demonstrate higher truth right in front of someone, when your presence reflects back to them all the limiting beliefs they've been choosing to believe to be true their entire life, and they begin to realize those beliefs aren't true anymore because they're witnessing something that defies what they thought was possible, it can be deeply uncomfortable for them. That's what was happening between me and Bob. I was shaking his foundation to the core, challenging everything he believed to be true. He couldn't deny what he witnessed in me, yet he tried to dismiss it as psychosis. He openly told me and others several times that I needed medication. I knew better and I never discriminated him for discriminating me, I had nothing but love for him. In truth it was one of the greatest blessings Bob ever gave me. On a Soul level I know Bob and I made this agreement before incarnation, that he would play this role so I could learn through contrast. For him to choose a life path of such polarity, to be my mirror and teacher through those circumstances, was an act of profound love. Bob is a master being. He simply hasn't remembered it yet.

One day my intuition told me to go to his house. I knew I'd have to endure discrimination from him and everyone there who shared his beliefs about me. I sat in his chair while waves of fear frequency were projected toward me. It appeared overwhelming and extremely challenging, at least from the perspective of who I used to be. But in that moment, I chose to perceive it neutrally, sitting there pleasantly and positively, maintaining blissfulness within myself. I didn't form opinions about what anyone said. I simply understood that it was their own fear being projected outward. By choosing not to have a problem with him for discriminating against me, by not judging or rejecting him, I was transmuting the energy in real time. Through that experience I was facing all six core fears at once: the fear of being uncomfortable, of what others choose to think and feel, of not being in control of my circumstance, of inadequacy, of lacking or losing, and of being alone. After losing my father Bob became like family, and one of my deepest fears was losing him. He'd had heart issues, and he always said he wanted me to give his eulogy someday. The thought terrified me. The idea of losing him felt unbearable. So when the household projected all that fear onto me, that old fear of loss surfaced again, one of the final fears I had to transcend.

As I sat there, feeling the intensity of it all, something extraordinary began happening. My body filled with euphoria, waves of bliss flooding through me, greater than any high I had ever known. Even as they were projecting fear, speaking words that most people would consider hurtful, expressing their limiting beliefs and trying to convince me to believe them so they could maintain a sense of familiarity and control, I remained in bliss. The energy built to such an intensity that my eyes closed on their own, and I fell into the longest *Samadhi* state I had ever experienced. All that fear and low vibration they were projecting became fuel. By fully accepting it, surrendering, and refusing to let it affect my state of being, I transmuted all of it. I turned that dense energy into fuel for ascension, using it as propulsion to lift my vibration upward until my *Sahasrara* fully opened. I fell into *Samadhi* for five hours. It was spontaneous. Unlike my previous *Samadhi* experiences, this time I hadn't even tried to meditate. The energy built and built until my Consciousness expanded beyond the physical body. That *Samadhi* was the most profound experience of my life, and the state of blissfulness that arose from it has continued long after I opened my eyes. In that state my *Pranamaya Kosha* became so radiant that my physical body followed suit. I began to heal physically, the infected wounds from injection sites began to close, cavities reversed, my mouth was healing. The energy of *Kundalini* makes healing possible in ways that transcend the understanding of Western science.

When I finally opened my eyes Bob had already told me to get out, that he never wanted to see me again. Yet the fear I once had of losing him no longer had any hold over me. I saw through the illusion of separation. I realized Bob and I are Soul family, two expressions of the same Consciousness. That version of me had chosen that life path to help this version of me experience awakening. I felt only unconditional love for Bob, and for all beings, all life, all of existence. I experienced all of existence as myself. I literally became love, the fundamental frequency that sustains the Universe and All That Is. I hugged Bob, told him I had nothing but love for him, thanked him, and walked out the door.

Since then Bob and I have reconnected. We may not be as close as we once were, but he's chosen to dissolve many of his limiting beliefs. By not discriminating against me anymore, and by me always loving and supporting him unconditionally, we've kept the door open between us. Even though we rarely speak and I now travel the world, the door is always open. The love is always there. I'll always be eternally grateful for Bob. He truly is one of my greatest teachers. He's a powerful, masterful being, and I have endless love for him.

That experience didn't just reveal the power of love between two Souls, it showed me what it truly means to embody love itself. It revealed to me the full truth of love's embodiment. When fear dissolves completely, only love remains, flowing effortlessly through every action and circumstance. From that moment forward, even the simplest experiences of daily life became an expression of the same stillness, the same presence, the same love I experienced in *Samadhi*.

Perfectly capable of doing everything, more than I've ever been, yet no longer feeling the need or desire to do anything, except simply to be. To allow my frequency to radiate in every direction, transmuting fear through all my circumstances wherever it touches. Raising the vibration of Consciousness on the planet simply by holding a frequency, simply by maintaining my state of being.

It doesn't come down to physical activity. Physical activity is only the surface level. The real miracle that's playing out can't be seen with the eyes, but rather perceived through intuition, synchronicity, and vibration. Real mastery isn't about reading all the ancient texts or all the spiritual books. It isn't about being able to perform the advanced *Asanas* on your yoga mat. It isn't about how much you go to church, how much you pray, or how long you meditate. Spirituality isn't about practice or ritual. Fundamentally, it's the willingness to break all the self-imposed limitations of the body and the mind and just be. True mastery is simply being in total presence. In that presence, the illusion of progress dissolves, and what remains is eternal becoming, without movement, without time.

Once you no longer feel the need or desire to control anything, once you no longer believe that you need anything, the Universe rewards you with everything. It's only once you become nothing that you can become everything. It's only once you no longer believe or desire that you need anything that you gain everything. The more you embody love and master your state of being, the more you become who you truly are. The more in alignment you become with your core vibrational frequency, you allow all the things in your life that are already working their way to you to get to you faster.

It's like you become this very strong magnet and you attract everything that you need in exact divine timing, not a moment too soon, not a moment too late, and all you have to do is maintain your awareness in the ever-expanding now. If you do the now really well, by maintaining total involvement and absolute awareness in the present moment, in the ever-expanding now, the future takes care of itself. All you have to do is simply be. When you live from this awareness, love begins to express itself through action, not as effort, but as effortless service. You don't have to go looking for ways to serve. Life brings them to you. Each moment becomes an invitation to express love in physical form, to be the embodiment of love in motion.

One thing I learned from my experience is that the more I offered myself in service to every given moment, doing whatever was needed in the moment, whatever my circumstance called for, the more I sustained this state of blissfulness, and the more the Universe took care of me, the more doors the Universe opened for me. One example I can give is when I was in Texas visiting some family at an event. While sitting there, I got the impulse that I needed to leave and walk outside. Of course, me being yes and yes, I happily obliged. I excused myself and went outside, where I found a lady who needed assistance. Her car had broken down in the parking lot. She was with her son, and their car had stopped on an incline, blocking part of the road. I told her I'd be happy to help. I ran back inside, grabbed three guys, and we went outside to push the car up the incline into the lot. The incline was too steep, and we couldn't make it. The others went back inside, and I stayed outside talking with her. When I asked how far her home was, she said just a few miles away. I told her I had AAA, which included a few free tows each year, and I'd call a tow truck for her.

The tow truck arrived and brought her car home. She was extremely grateful, almost in disbelief that a complete stranger would go out of their way to help without expecting anything in return. She appreciated it so much that she invited me to dinner. It was a beautiful opportunity to connect, and of course I accepted, because I'm yes and yes. We met at a restaurant and began talking. She asked about my life, and of course I'm not one for small talk. I don't remain on the surface level. I go deep. I told her about my awakening and what I'd been realizing from it. She said it felt like divine intervention that our paths crossed, because she'd recently been exploring meditation and had several questions. I was happy to answer and offer her clarity.

I inspired her to follow her highest excitement, raise her vibration, and transcend fear, all because I said yes and yes to the impulse to leave the event and go outside. I didn't care if it seemed rude or inconvenient. I just followed my inner guidance and met a beautiful being who needed help, not only circumstantially but internally. That's what excites me most, helping others break the limitations they've imposed on themselves. Helping their Consciousness grow and expand so they can experience unity with Source and remember that they are All That Is. Nothing excites me more.

When you maintain your state of being in your highest frequency of authenticity by embodying love, the organizing principle of reality, which is synchronicity, manifests circumstances to support you so you can continue to act on your highest excitement. All you have to do is follow the guidance without expectation of the outcome. Choose to stay in a positive, pleasant state no matter what manifests. See the silver lining in everything and attach a positive definition to all of your circumstances. When you do this, you dissolve the belief systems that aren't in alignment with who you truly are. That's how you sustain your highest frequency of authenticity. That's how you embody love. The more you live this way, the more you realize that every act of service, no matter how small, is a reflection of the same infinite love. The Universe continues to give you new opportunities to dissolve fear and express that love in different forms.

Another example I can give that demonstrates this truth is what happens when you no longer buy into the fear of the imagination, the fear of security, survival, of lacking or losing. When you no longer vibrate with scarcity consciousness or a low vibration, but instead choose to maintain your highest frequency of authenticity and love by simply being in every given moment, your circumstances no longer influence you. The Universe is always testing us, giving us more and more opportunities to transcend the same six fears. It's a never-ending thing. We simply create new circumstances with different paint jobs of a higher vibrational outcome to transcend the same six fears over and over again.

One day, I saw some people living on the street. They looked hungry. I walked over to them, gave one man a big hug, and said, "How you doing today?" Then I laughed and said, "Or no, how are you choosing to be today?" He looked at me and said, "Man, I'm just struggling out here. Nothing seems to be going right." I said, "Well, I can't fix all your circumstances, but I'd be happy to buy you a meal." I pulled out my wallet and gave him the last twenty-dollar bill I had to my name. I didn't get stuck in my imagination, worrying about how I was going to eat dinner that night, how I was going to come up with more money, or how I'd be able to support myself. Those thoughts never even crossed my mind. In that moment, I simply did whatever was needed, whatever the circumstance called for, willingly and happily, while maintaining my highest frequency of authenticity, exuding nothing but bliss, love, and gratitude.

I gave him my last twenty dollars and sat with him for a while. We didn't say much. We just enjoyed the silence together and each other's presence. He was a beautiful being. I could feel the love and gratitude coming from him, and the disbelief that someone would walk up, give him a hug, ask how he was doing, and then give him the last bit of money they had. By doing this, by transcending the fear of lacking and losing, I kept my vibration high and helped him raise his vibration, which is the only thing I actually care about. That's what my highest excitement always is, helping others raise their vibration.

The Universe blessed me once again. Later that same day, someone handed me an envelope with five hundred dollars cash in it. I absolutely wasn't expecting it. It appeared on the surface to be completely random, but of course I understand that nothing is random. Everything is perfectly orchestrated, like a beautiful symphony of vibration.

Everything that unfolds in your reality is designed to help you remember who you are. Every circumstance, every interaction, and every challenge is an invitation to embody love more fully. The more you align with your vibration of authenticity, by embodying love, the more effortlessly life flows. When you embody love, there's no separation between the spiritual and the physical, between Heaven and Earth, between self and other. It all becomes one seamless expression of Consciousness, endlessly creating, endlessly becoming. Love is the bridge between all dimensions. It's the fabric of reality itself. It's the vibration through which Source experiences creation. When you live in remembrance of this, you stop searching for meaning and start expressing it through your being. You realize that the highest service you can offer the world is the frequency you hold within yourself. Every thought, every breath, every heartbeat becomes an offering to the whole. When you embody love, you don't have to speak about it, you radiate it. You don't have to prove it, you live it. You don't have to seek it, you are it. In the stillness of being, the whole Universe recognizes itself through you.

CLOSING REFLECTION

The embodiment of love is not a path you walk, it's the awareness that you are the path itself. When you rest in this awareness, life becomes sacred. Every breath is *Sadhana*, every step is creation, and every encounter becomes an opportunity to reflect the light of love. Love doesn't need to be achieved or sought. It reveals itself in the absence of effort. The more you surrender to what is, the more love expresses through you without resistance. It heals without trying, gives without expecting, and teaches without words. To embody love is to return to your natural state of being, to remember that you are already whole. Nothing is missing, nothing is separate, and nothing needs to be done. You are the movement and the stillness, the giver and the gift, the presence through which the Universe knows itself as love.

TRANSMISSION 11

MANIFESTATION THROUGH ALIGNMENT

Manifestation isn't about forcing reality to change. It's about aligning with the version of reality that already exists in resonance with your vibration. In this transmission we'll explore how reality itself is structured through frequency, how manifestation truly works, and how your state of being determines everything you experience in the ever-expanding now.

The illusion of reality appears to be solid. It appears to be continuous, but it's not. We experience time in a linear fashion in this density of Consciousness, the Third ascending into the Fourth density of Consciousness. In actuality there's only one moment, the ever-expanding now. If you think of it like the cinema analogy, when the filmstrip is being run through the projector and the light is shining through, the images that get projected onto the wall appear to move seamlessly with perfect continuity. But that's actually an illusion. If you look at the filmstrip itself, you can see that it's simply individual frames being projected rapidly through the light. That's what creates the illusion of movement and continuity.

Reality works the same way. Your Consciousness is phasing over a billion times per second through over a billion different parallel realities. Since the changes between each of these frames are so subtle and because the shifting happens so fast, you don't perceive the difference. You experience it as a continuous flowing moment. That's the illusion of time. Higher density beings don't experience time in a linear fashion because their awareness is expanded enough to see the entire filmstrip at once. They can look at any frame, any version of reality they choose, and experience it fully, not as memory, not as imagination, but as living presence. They can shift their focus to any frequency and live that frame completely. We haven't yet evolved to that level of awareness. Here on Earth we're still in the school of Third density Consciousness, ascending into Fourth, the realm of unity and love, moving beyond separation and division.

Manifestation works through alignment, coherence, and vibration. Some of the ancient indigenous tribes knew this. Their awareness, intuition, and connection with nature and the divine were far less distorted than those of modern civilizations. They remembered something that their ancestors had preserved through their culture, that reality mirrors vibration. Let's say you're a farmer. You're farming your field to feed your family, but this season there's been a drought. No rain. Fear starts to arise, fear of survival, fear of security. How will you feed your family without water for your crops? When you vibrate in fear, you're unconsciously broadcasting that frequency into the Universe. You pray, please God let it rain. But what you're really saying vibrationally is, it's not raining. You're focusing on the lack. The Universe doesn't respond to words, it responds to frequency. Whatever you're vibrating at now is what you'll experience.

So when you vibrate from lack, you attract more lack. When you vibrate from abundance, you attract more abundance. The Universe is unconditional. It always mirrors back to you exactly what you're choosing to be in this moment. These indigenous people understood this. When a rainmaker does a dance or ritual to call the rain, the ritual itself doesn't cause the rain. The ritual is a permission slip for the subconscious mind, a symbolic act that helps the mind believe that rain is possible. The true power lies in Consciousness. The ritual only helps get the person out of their own way.

So imagine you're that farmer again. You go out to your field, but instead of worrying, you sit down in the soil, close your eyes, and bring yourself completely into the present moment. You imagine that it's already raining. You feel every drop hitting your face, running down your cheeks. You feel your hair and clothes getting wet. You sense the pressure change in the air, the smell of rain in the wind, the sound of the thunder rolling in the distance. You can hear every drop bouncing off the leaves and soil. You even taste the rain as it drips from your lips. You hold this vision with complete focus and gratitude, as if it's happening now. Your subconscious mind doesn't know the difference between imagination and reality, because your thoughts create reality. The longer you stay in that state, the more coherent your vibration becomes. Greater coherence means your shift into that parallel reality becomes more immediate in your physical experience. The Universe feels what you feel. When you feel gratitude for the rain that already is, the Universe aligns with that vibration. It has no choice. It must reflect that reality back to you.

Sometimes physical reality seems to lag because of its density. It may take a few frames of the filmstrip before your senses perceive the change. Once your vibration is coherent, the shift happens instantly in Consciousness. You don't make it rain. You shift to the version of reality where the circumstances are vibrationally aligned with your intention and gratitude for it already raining. That's how manifestation through alignment and coherence works.

After my *Samadhi* experiences, I stayed in the same state of total surrender that had allowed them to happen. That surrender soon expressed itself in a very practical way. I gave away all my possessions, all my money, everything I thought I needed to survive, and yet I felt more alive and fulfilled than ever before. I was realizing how reality truly responds to vibration, how manifestation isn't about effort but about alignment. I remember one day when all I wanted was a small blow-up pillow so that when I went out into the countryside to meditate, I could sit comfortably without my body getting wet from the grass. That was it, something so simple. While meditating in my mother's spare room, I found myself naturally visualizing it. I was sitting by a lake in the countryside, the sun warm on my face, the sound of fish jumping out of the water, the gentle rustling of leaves in the wind. I could feel the humidity in the air, the scent of summer grass, the softness of the pillow beneath me. It felt completely real, even more vivid than waking reality. I held that visualization unwaveringly for what felt like several minutes, fully immersed, feeling absolute gratitude for simply being alive, not once feeling lack or need. When I finally opened my eyes, I felt an intuitive impulse to go for a walk, so being yes and yes, that's exactly what I did.

Synchronicities were flowing so clearly and so constantly at that time that it felt as though I was living inside a lucid dream. Every moment shimmered with meaning, reflecting my vibration with perfect precision. It was overwhelming and beautiful all at once, like walking through magic that had suddenly become visible. I followed the energy the way you follow a stream uphill, simply letting it guide me. After a couple of miles, I reached a lake near my mother's house, a beach that was usually packed full of people, but that day it was empty. I walked along the shore toward a tree where I often liked to sit and meditate, and there it was, a perfect little blow-up pillow sitting under the tree waiting. I laughed out loud. It was exactly what I had envisioned. At first I thought, how could this be, but deep down I already knew. I had manifested it. How it arrived there didn't matter. Whether someone left it behind or it literally materialized out of thin air made no difference to me. The Universe had placed it there in perfect alignment with the vibration I was putting out. I was overwhelmed with gratitude.

That happened because my Consciousness shifted to the version of reality where that pillow already existed under that tree. Since my focus had been so clear, unwavering, and sustained during that visualization, my vibration anchored into the parallel reality that matched that frequency. The impulse to go for a walk was simply the Universe's way of saying, you're now fully aligned, go receive it.

Soon after that, similar manifestations began happening faster and faster, appearing almost like magic. During that same time, as I was moving around in my car with no home of my own, I started imagining how nice it would be to have a tent so that I could sleep more comfortably. I visualized myself inside that tent, surrounded by stillness and peace, feeling safe, feeling at home wherever I was. After about half an hour of visualizing, I opened my eyes and overheard the people I was staying with talking about their friend who was coming over that night to camp in the yard with their kids. I said how amazing that sounded and that I'd love to join but didn't have a tent. Instantly my friend looked at me and said, we have an extra one, you can have it. I was amazed but not surprised. I knew exactly what had happened.

Later, I wanted to make that tent feel like a real home, so I started visualizing again, this time an area rug inside, something soft and warm that would fill the tent's floor so that it felt cozy and inviting. I didn't imagine exactly what it looked like; I just held the feeling of gratitude, of comfort, of being at peace in that space. When I came out of meditation, I got the impulse to drive back to my old apartment one last time to clear out the few bags of garbage and clothes I had left behind in the garage. I followed that impulse without question. When I opened the garage door, there it was, a beautiful area rug I had never seen before. I had no idea how it got there, and I didn't care. I threw away the trash, grabbed the rug, and drove back to my friends smiling the entire way. When I set up my tent and unrolled the rug, it fit perfectly, to the inch, as though it had been made specifically for that tent.

That moment showed me again how manifestation really works. My Consciousness had shifted to the version of reality where the rug already existed. The impulse to drive back to my old apartment was the Universe's way of saying you're now aligned with the reality mirroring your vibration, go receive your gift.

When I trust those impulses, when I follow my intuition and stay in gratitude, the Universe always takes care of me.

As I kept living in my car, I refused to bathe anywhere that used city water. I was deeply conscious of what I was putting in and on my body, especially while I was healing myself naturally, so I only bathed in lakes. That whole time I moved all around Minnesota, the land of ten thousand lakes, exploring as many as I could, swimming in them, meditating beside them, and feeling their stillness. Every lake felt sacred. Each time I entered the water it wasn't just a bath, it was a return to purity, a merging with Source through nature.

One afternoon I found this beautiful lake somewhere outside of the Twin Cities. I can't remember its name now, but I can still see it in my mind, peaceful, glimmering under the sun, the breeze whispering softly through the trees. I grabbed my yoga mat, found a shady spot under a tree, and started to meditate. After a while, I got the clear impulse, that inner voice, telling me to jump in the lake. At first I hesitated, because even though it was warm outside, I knew the water would be cold. When I opened my eyes, I noticed the dock had a railing all the way around, which would make it hard to climb back out once I jumped in. My mind immediately started making excuses, but the voice kept repeating itself, jump in the lake, jump in the lake, jump in the lake.

Eventually I said to myself, all right, I will, but I need a towel first. I walked back to my car and started searching. I tore everything apart, checking every corner and under every seat, but there wasn't a towel anywhere. It made no sense. I always had at least one or two with me. Everything I owned was in my car, and they had just been with me the day before, and yet they had completely disappeared. The whole time I kept hearing the voice, louder and louder, jump in the lake, jump in the lake. Finally I gave up and said out loud, fine, I don't need a towel, I'll go jump in the lake.

When I got back to the dock, I noticed there was no one around. Just a few people having a picnic up on a hill, but no one near the water. I set my phone, wallet, and car keys on the railing by the dock. Those were all I owned at the time. My phone was a gift from my mom so she could stay in touch with me, and my wallet had the little money I had left. If someone came along and took them while I was in the water, I'd be stranded with nothing. But in that moment, I completely surrendered. I looked at my things sitting there and thought, if someone takes them, then so be it. I trust. I took a deep breath, ran as fast as I could down the dock, and dove headfirst over the railing into the water.

The cold hit me instantly, but instead of shock, I felt completely alive. It was pure life rushing through me. I rolled onto my back and floated there, feeling the warmth of the sun on my face, the cool water holding me, the birds singing above, the gentle sound of the ripples around me. I lost all sense of time. Gratitude filled every part of me, for the sun, for the water, for the stillness, for existence itself. There was no separation between me and the lake, between me and the Universe. Everything was one field of being, one presence.

I don't know how long I floated there, but when I finally opened my eyes and swam back to the dock, I saw something that stopped me in my tracks. Draped neatly over the railing, right next to my phone, wallet, and keys, was a brand new towel. It hadn't been there before. There was no one around. It was just there, waiting for me. I stared at it, completely still, completely in awe. I climbed up onto the dock, picked it up, and smiled. I didn't question it. I didn't need to. I already knew what had happened.

That towel was the Universe's way of showing me that when I truly follow my intuition, when I trust those inner impulses without hesitation, the Universe supports me completely. The more I surrendered and trusted, the more miracles appeared. Each one reflected my willingness to live in alignment with my higher vibration, to say yes to the unknown. When you master your state of being and no longer let fear, doubt, or lack control your life, the Universe provides for you in ways the mind can't comprehend. Everything you need arrives in perfect timing, and the more you say yes, the more life says yes to you.

One main problem people have with manifestation is impatience. It all starts with intention. They put an intention out into the Universe, but because they carry an unconscious belief system, an expectation about how that intention is supposed to manifest in physical reality, it limits them and it limits the Universe's possibilities of how it can manifest for them. It's like taking an infinite number of possibilities, a number so vast the human brain can't even comprehend it, and narrowing it all the way down to one single possibility. I want this, and I want the Universe to manifest it exactly like this. That's one of the biggest reasons people struggle to manifest.

They set an intention, but they don't stay in alignment with it. They think, a couple of weeks, a couple of months, even a few years have gone by, and it still hasn't materialized in physical reality, so they move their awareness, drop that intention, and shift their focus to something else. What happens when you do this is that you're putting out conflicting frequencies into the Universe. The Universe wants nothing more than to align for you and manifest literally everything you desire, but it's all done through vibration. When you put a vibration out, an intention, as long as your thoughts, emotions, and actions stay aligned with it, it has to manifest in physical reality. Be patient.

Most people aren't willing to stay in that alignment because it doesn't happen in the way they expect, or they hold limiting beliefs that it's not possible. Physical reality is lagged. It's a dense version of Consciousness. It's slow. It can take time for things to manifest, to fully take form in the physical world. There are countless moving parts that all need to align perfectly, like a living orchestra of frequency, each note harmonizing with the next in divine precision, so that the one thing you're trying to manifest can come into resonance with this infinite ocean of vibration. That single frequency of your manifestation has to align with your individualized Consciousness.

How you manifest abundance in all forms is through the willingness to do whatever is needed in the moment. That's the key. What I've learned from my own experience of being yes and yes, of living with that level of willingness, is that this is exactly how it all works. When you're willing to do whatever is needed in the moment, whatever your circumstance calls for, and when you put your personal wants and desires aside to make your life a complete offering in service to others, the Universe blesses you and takes care of you in ways that defy the mind.

Your life becomes one continuous miracle, blessing after

blessing, manifestation after manifestation, all unfolding in perfect divine timing. It's always mirroring back to you what you're vibrating within yourself. When you truly live from the frequency of abundance instead of the frequency of lack, you naturally do whatever is needed in the moment without hesitation and without fear. When you maintain that vibration, that state of being, the Universe mirrors it back to you, and infinite possible manifestations begin to take form in physical reality once you're out of your own way.

The simplest way to manifest abundance in all forms is through the willingness to do whatever is needed in the moment. That's what it means to be yes and yes. It's removing *no* from your vocabulary and saying yes to life, yes to growth, and yes to the guidance of the Universe. Living this way opens you completely to the infinite possibilities that already exist in the ever-expanding now. Being yes and yes is the vibration of alignment and the frequency of trust. It means you're no longer resisting life or trying to control how things unfold. You begin to respond consciously to what each moment asks of you, doing whatever is needed with presence, gratitude, and love. This is how abundance flows, not through forcing or chasing, but through allowing and aligning.

Your state of being determines everything. Whatever you're vibrating at now is exactly what you attract. When your thoughts, emotions, and beliefs harmonize as one, your vibration becomes coherent. If you're putting out the vibration of lack, you'll experience more lack. If you're putting out the vibration of abundance, gratitude, and trust, you'll experience abundance in all forms. This is the most essential understanding of manifestation. Every experience in your life is a mirror of your own frequency. The Universe isn't separate from you; it reflects you. It hears not your words but your vibration, arranging circumstances through synchronicities to show you what you're vibrating at right now.

Living in full alignment, as yes and yes, constantly aligns your Consciousness with the realities that match your vibration. Choosing to remain in a positive and pleasant state, no matter what your circumstance is, shifts you into a version of reality that reflects that same frequency back to you. Manifestation works through vibration and alignment in the ever-expanding now, not through effort or control. The more you trust, the more you allow, and the more you say yes to the moment before you, the more effortlessly the Universe flows through you. In that flow, every experience becomes abundance itself.

CLOSING REFLECTION

Manifestation isn't something you do. It's something you allow. The more you relax into what is, the more you align with what's already becoming. The Universe doesn't respond to effort, it responds to frequency. You don't have to chase, control, or convince. You only have to become the vibration of what you wish to experience. You are the portal through which reality takes form. The moment you remember that, you realize that everything you desire already exists in the field of now, waiting for you to come into coherence with it.

Be grateful for what already is. Gratitude is the bridge between what seems to be and what's becoming. When you give thanks before the manifestation appears, you're telling the Universe, "I already have it," and that truth magnetizes it to you with effortless precision. Trust that every breath, every delay, every redirection is love guiding you toward the most aligned version of yourself. What is for you can never pass you by.

So keep saying yes and yes. Keep meeting each moment as the only moment there is. Keep trusting the current that carries you through the infinite ocean of realities, knowing that you're never separate from what you seek. You are the rainmaker, the dreamer, the dream, and the sky it unfolds within. When you live from that knowing, life itself becomes the miracle.

TRANSMISSION 12

FEAR'S FINAL ILLUSION

The final veil between you and the infinite is the illusion that you were ever separate at all.

The ego isn't real. It doesn't exist. It's nothing more than a facade, a series of belief systems you're choosing to believe to be true about yourself, things you identify with, that you believe define you. I am Tyson. I am a man. I am Caucasian. When we identify with things, it causes us to experience the illusion of separation from Source. The more things you identify with, the stronger that separation feels. The ego is the part of you that always feels it has to be right or be heard. It feels it needs to defend or argue because it's coming from fear. Most of the time when I speak of ego, I relate it directly to fear. That's what most people understand ego to be as well. For the sake of conversation, it's easier to think of it like that. Ego means fear, fear frequency. Ego is what causes the illusion of separation. It makes you believe there's a difference between you and me. But there's also a positive ego, the aspect of self that remains after awakening, the personality that's in full service to the divine, to the Universe.

Without the ego, there would be no sense of individualized self. Without a sense of individualized self, there would be no way for Consciousness to experience itself as a human being. When I use the word "ego" throughout these transmissions, I'm referring to the fear-based aspect of the ego, the false identity that believes it's separate from Source. This is the aspect of ego that's meant to dissolve for Unity to be realized. The positive ego simply lets Consciousness navigate physical reality. It's the part of self that maintains individuality and coordination within the illusion of time and space while still serving the greater Whole. All ego is a collection of belief systems that Consciousness chooses to experience through physical form. When those beliefs are aligned with your true vibration, the ego serves as a clear expression of love. When those beliefs are rooted in fear or separation, the ego becomes limiting and creates the illusion of separation from Source. Physical reality itself is literally a projection of Consciousness, built on the belief systems you're choosing to believe to be true. If you had absolutely no belief systems, you wouldn't exist in human form.

You've probably heard the saying, if you want to change the world, you first have to change yourself. This saying rings true on multiple levels. You never actually change your world, you change your vibration, and therefore you change the parallel reality you experience. Your Consciousness shifts to the reality that matches what you're choosing to vibrate at. If you want to change the mirror your world shows back to you, you must first change yourself. Be the walking, living example of what you wish to see in the world, not just through your actions but through the vibration behind them. Life doesn't mirror what you do, it mirrors what you are, the frequency you embody.

What's often called ego death is simply the dissolving of all belief systems that aren't in alignment with your Higher Self, all the fear-based beliefs that are causing the illusion of separation from Source. The more someone chooses to raise their vibration by transcending fear and dissolving limiting beliefs, the more the ego dissolves. But the ego itself never truly existed; it can be dissolved in a single moment. It doesn't have to be a long process. You don't need to go to healing retreats or sign up for therapy unless you believe you need to. There's nothing wrong with that. Those modalities can be extremely beneficial in the right moment for the right individual. Healing works the same way. The moment you choose to be healed, the shift can happen instantly. Fundamentally, everything is a choice.

You choose how you want to be in every given moment based on the belief systems you're choosing to believe to be true. All it takes is one moment of absolute willingness to let everything go, everything you identify with, every belief system that limits you and distorts your frequency, every illusion of separation. One moment of complete surrender. When you drop all identities and no longer choose to believe to be true all the nonsense you've been perpetuating in your mind your entire life, in that single moment you can fall into a state of *Samadhi* and remember who and what you truly are.

The ego doesn't want to give up control. It gets comfortable in familiarity. It doesn't care how dysfunctional or toxic your life circumstances appear to be. It wants to maintain familiarity. Since it's fear, it wants to contract. It wants to keep you limited because then it can stay in control. It doesn't want you to expand. Like I've said before, the whole point of this human experience in this school we call Earth, in the third dimension, in the Third density of Consciousness, is to ascend to the Fourth density of Consciousness. The Third density of Consciousness is the experience of separation and division, which is what most people here on planet Earth are experiencing right now. A large part of the population is going through an ascension phase, moving from Third density to Fourth density. Fourth density is all about unity and love.

Fourth density is when it has come into your awareness through direct realization that you're not just a being. When you become aware that you are the entire Universe, the seen and the unseen. You are all of existence, Source choosing to have a human experience. You are All That Is. There's absolutely nothing wrong with you. You are Source choosing to have a human experience, and Source doesn't make mistakes. Every experience, every emotion, every choice you've ever made has been perfect. It's all been part of your awakening, part of your remembrance. You came here to experience it all, the light and the dark, the pleasure and the pain, to remember through contrast who and what you truly are. You're not broken. You don't need fixing. You're the infinite remembering itself as you. Having that realization is the ascension from Third density to Fourth density. That evolution in Consciousness is the whole point of why we signed up for this school called Earth.

Earth is a tough school. It's a master class. Only advanced beings choose to incarnate on Earth because of the dramatic amount of self-imposed separation from Source that we choose to experience when we incarnate as a human being. Forgetting what we truly are when we come into physical form. Not even remembering that we ever existed before. Believing that we are this limited human being in this body, in this narrative that plays in our head, that we identify with as me. That whole process of going from that extreme amount of separation and limitation to experiencing boundlessness and limitlessness, to having your Consciousness expand from the focal point within your body infinitely in every direction, and having the realization that you literally are All That Is. All is One.

The ego will do everything it can to deceive you, to trick you into continuing to believe the nonsensical limiting beliefs that you've been believing your whole life. The closer you get to discovering a core belief that's been limiting you, the more resistance you'll feel within yourself, and the more fear will be projected into your circumstances. The closer you get to dissolving a core belief that's been majorly limiting you, the more intense it can seem. This happens because the ego doesn't want you to discover the core belief, so it'll compulsively create five new limiting beliefs to distract you, to keep you preoccupied so you don't figure out the core belief. Once you figure out the core belief and choose to dissolve it, once you choose to no longer believe it to be true, you redefine it in a positive way that serves you in the way you prefer. That's how you kill the ego. That's how you dissolve the negative ego, and it doesn't want to be dissolved.

If your circumstances ever appear to be very intense or filled with fear, don't be scared of that. Don't fear fear. Remember, fear is the compass always guiding you home to your Higher Self. The scarier it gets, put your hands together, bow down to it, and be grateful for it. You realize that it must get scarier right before the breakthrough, before the expansion, when you finally see that there's nothing to be scared of. It's just constructs in your mind that you've been choosing to believe to be true. Be grateful for the fear. Be grateful for the ego. Don't try to run from it or deny it. Be grateful for it, transmute it, dissolve it, and let it go. That's how you expand your Consciousness. Whatever emotion you're feeling in any given moment, whatever thoughts you're having, there's absolutely nothing wrong with any of it. It's essential that you own your feelings.

If you're experiencing an emotion that you don't prefer, don't try to bury it or deny it. Don't try to lock it up in a box because you're too scared to look at it or face it. That's the worst thing you could do to yourself. Face that fear. Look directly at that part of yourself and ask, what am I choosing to believe to be true that would make me believe I have to feel this way? Ask yourself, what am I so scared of? What is it that I'm actually so scared of? What's the worst possible thing that could happen? By being inquisitive like this, you help reveal the illusion of fear instead of letting the mental diarrhea, the endless noise of memory and imagination looping between past and future, go off on a tangent. When you face the fear head-on, you can discover the belief system you've been choosing to believe to be true and let it go.

When you're having a thought or emotion that you don't prefer, there's nothing wrong with that. Anything you're ever choosing to feel in any given moment is perfectly okay. There's no such thing as right or wrong. There's no such thing as good or bad, or positive or negative. Those are all constructs of the mind that limit us and make us experience more of the illusion of separation from Source. Whatever you're feeling, own your feelings and understand that the only reason you might be choosing to suffer over it is because you have a belief system that's making you believe you have to. All you have to do is apply the process to it. When you do that, that's how you transmute the fear. That's how you change the energy by changing the belief system or dissolving it completely. When you do that, you raise your vibration, and that starts the manifestation process of new circumstances that are in alignment with your new vibration.

It's a continuing, never-ending process. It doesn't matter how much someone raises their vibration or what type of higher states of Consciousness someone's been able to experience. The fundamentals are always the same. It's always there to teach you to transcend fear, to continuously raise your vibration. If you think of it as school, you have a kindergartner and a twelfth grader. Both of them are beings, and neither one of them is better than the other. They're both the same. The only difference is the kindergartner started school after the twelfth grader. The twelfth grader has more experience and has evolved through the other grades, while the kindergartner is just starting out. The twelfth grader isn't going to expect the kindergartner to know advanced algebra. The twelfth grader's going to make sure the kindergartner is safe and knows where the classroom is. The twelfth grader will hold the hand of the kindergartner and walk that child to their class to make sure they get where they're supposed to go. If you think of Consciousness like that, everybody evolves at their own pace. There's nothing wrong with anything or anyone ever. If someone has more awareness within themselves than someone else, it doesn't mean they're better than them. They're the same. They're simply another version of you.

If you have more awareness, if you've been able to embody love and you understand this process, you can realize that at one point in time, you were also unconscious, compulsive, and reactive. So have compassion for others when you see them exhibiting that behavior. When you see them unconsciously choosing to suffer, meet them with love, meet them with acceptance, meet them with total compassion and unconditional support. Have absolutely no expectations of them or of yourself, because expectation is always the root of all suffering. As you begin to awaken more fully, you realize that every experience in this school is an opportunity to expand in love. Every person who crosses your path is both teacher and reflection. Awareness is what turns experience into wisdom, but compassion is what turns wisdom into unity. One of the simplest and most powerful ways to remember this truth is through a shift in perception that reveals the unity already present in all of life.

Another simple technique that can help you become more conscious and raise your awareness into compassion, love, understanding, and acceptance is to begin seeing every being you encounter as yourself. Choose to look at every single person, every single life form, as another version of you, because it is you in a different form, wearing a different body, speaking through a different voice. Don't look at anyone as separate from you, not even as a separate Soul. See them literally as you. When you begin to do this, judgment starts to dissolve and the illusion of separation weakens. If you were looking at yourself in the mirror and you asked yourself for help, would you help yourself? Of course you would. You'd respond with compassion, patience, understanding, and acceptance. You'd give exactly what was needed in the moment without hesitation or condition. This is how you're meant to treat everyone and everything in life, not only every human being, but every expression of life itself. Every tree, every bee, every bird, every cat, every dog, every ant, every spider, even the cockroaches. Before you lift your foot to step on one, realize that it too is another version of you in a different form, playing a different part in the grand play of existence.

When you begin to truly see this way, your entire reality starts to transform. You start to live from unity rather than division, from love rather than fear. This isn't imagination or belief. It's direct perception. It's what naturally unfolds after *Samadhi* when the sense of separateness dissolves completely. You no longer have to try to look at others this way. It becomes effortless, the only way you can perceive. But until that realization dawns, you can consciously use this technique as a doorway. Practice seeing all as self, and you begin to align your perception with the truth of unity, with the vibration of all-inclusiveness, and with love. When you begin living from this state of perception, life itself becomes a mirror of oneness. Every encounter shows you where love still wants to express itself through you. Every challenge becomes a chance to remember that you're never interacting with anyone but yourself. This is how the lessons of the school are mastered, not by escaping the classroom, but by realizing that the teacher, the student, and the lesson are all the same being in different forms.

Understanding these truths in theory is one thing, but

embodying them in real life is another. After my awakening, I was given the perfect opportunity to live this realization through a relationship that would teach me everything about love without expectation. Life, in its infinite intelligence, always brings you the perfect circumstances to practice this truth, sometimes through strangers, and sometimes through the people who touch your heart the deepest.

After my awakening, I became close with a woman we'll call Sarah. We didn't label or define our relationship. We both knew that the only way it would work was if we maintained absolutely zero expectations within ourselves and of each other. I supported her in whatever she wanted, and she supported me in whatever I wanted. We were perfect reflections, showing each other true authenticity. It was the healthiest relationship I'd ever had up to that point in my life. Before that, many of my relationships had appeared to be very toxic, but in truth, they were the greatest teachers of my life.

When I told her I was leaving to continue my journey, it was understandably challenging for her. I reminded her that the worst thing she could do was not do something out of fear of what I might think or feel about it. I told her that if she met someone and wanted to date them, she should do whatever she wanted and never ask for my permission. I reminded her that nothing can make me feel anything, that I always choose how I want to be in every given moment. I told her to always act on her highest excitement and not allow fear frequency to creep back in.

A couple of months later, we were still talking every day. One day she called me and told me she'd met someone named Frank who'd caught her interest. I told her she didn't need my permission, that she should be her authentic self and do whatever she wanted, and to choose to stay in a positive state no matter what manifested. When I left, a lot of her friends had started projecting their fears onto her. They told her that what we had wasn't a real or conventional relationship, that if I truly loved her, I wouldn't have left. They projected a lot of limiting beliefs onto her, and she chose to believe them to be true. She started to resonate with the fear frequency they were projecting.

She began dating this man, and one day she called and said she felt like she was being unauthentic to both me and Frank by talking to me while seeing him. I asked her, why are you choosing to feel that way? Why do you feel like you're doing something wrong or something bad? What belief system are you choosing to believe to be true that's limiting you and making you feel like you have to experience exclusion instead of inclusiveness? We never defined our relationship. It didn't need to be physical. It was just two beings truly enjoying each other's company and helping one another grow. Then one day, she suddenly cut off all communication. We went from talking every day to complete silence, and that was okay. I chose to stay in a positive, pleasant state because I remembered that I'd told her from the beginning, do whatever you want, I support you unconditionally.

Later on during my travels, months later, our paths crossed again. She answered the door, visibly uncomfortable. We sat at the table, and she began to cry. She said, "I'm so sorry I ghosted you like that." I smiled and said, "Sarah, it's okay. Why are you choosing to feel this way? You didn't do anything wrong. I told you I support you unconditionally. If you wanted to ghost me, I support that too." She told me I'd made her feel uncomfortable. I said, "No, I don't make you feel anything. You're choosing to feel uncomfortable. Why? What belief system are you choosing to believe to be true?" She asked, "What would you have done if Frank had been here?" I said, "What do you mean, what would I have done if Frank had been here?" I would've given him a hug and said thank you for being so good to Sarah, because she deserves it. I thought to myself, what's the problem here? I couldn't understand why she was choosing to make a problem out of this.

True love is all-inclusive. When fear appears in a relationship, it can show up in many ways. Sometimes it's projected from one person onto another, and other times it's created within your own imagination, often fueled by memory. Maybe Frank had his own insecurities or fears of inadequacy and projected those onto Sarah, and she chose to believe them to be true. Or maybe he never said anything at all, and Sarah's own fear of losing him, rooted in past experiences and memory, created that story in her mind and played out through her imagination. Either way, the circumstance itself doesn't matter. It's simply the same frequency of fear taking form through different reflections. There's nothing wrong with any of it. There's no such thing as right or wrong. Whatever someone's choosing to feel or act upon is perfectly okay. Whenever we choose to believe those fears and conform to them, we're simply matching that vibration and limiting our expansion.

People come into our life when it's relevant. When there's something for us to learn, we manifest individuals to come into our life. On the surface level, it can appear random, but of course it isn't. Our Higher Self orchestrates those circumstances to give the physical self, this version of you, and the new individual who's appeared in your life, that version of you, an opportunity to come together and learn from each other. To be the reflections that each other need in those moments, so both can grow, so both can expand in Consciousness and become more of their authentic self. When the lessons have been learned, and it's no longer relevant for that person to stay in your life, it's simply because on a Soul level, you've learned what you agreed to learn together. Once the lesson has been experienced, it might not be relevant to stay in physical proximity anymore. The realization of why they came into your life may unfold later, in its own time.

On the surface, it might look like a disagreement, a breakup, a move, or a new relationship. But vibrationally, it's simply the natural way frequency realigns itself. The ego wants you to believe that means failure, but it isn't. The relationship was a complete success. When two beings are no longer vibrating in harmony, they drift apart into new realities where their experiences may no longer overlap. Everyone evolves and expands at their own rate, and when one being is experiencing a faster acceleration than another, their wavelengths stop matching. It's not personal. It's not good or bad. It's simply the architecture of reality. It's how frequency resonates.

There's nothing wrong with any of this. There's no such thing as right or wrong. Everyone's life path is their own and completely unique. Everything that happens in your life is happening exactly as your Higher Self has planned for it to. I've been able to perceive this through every circumstance, which is why I've learned to surrender fully and accept everything exactly as it is, without forming opinions or choosing to have issues with it. I trust the highest form of my intelligence steering my life. That's what allows me to meet everyone, no matter where they are, with love, acceptance, and unconditional support. It's the recognition that we're all equal. Some of us have simply been in school a little longer.

CLOSING REFLECTION

The illusion of ego was never something to destroy. It was something to experience. The moment you recognize that fear and love are simply different frequencies of the same Source, you awaken from the dream of separation. You begin to see that even the ego, the shadow, the story, the mask, was never against you. It was always guiding you home. It played the role of resistance so you could remember what you really are.

The path of awakening isn't about becoming someone new. It's about letting go of everything you're not. The ego clings to identities and stories, believing that control equals safety. But safety is an illusion. Control is an illusion. You've never been anything other than infinite Consciousness pretending to be small for the joy of remembering its own vastness. When you finally stop running from yourself, when you stop trying to fix, chase, or prove, the running ends. The seeking ends. What remains is your natural state, stillness, bliss.

In that stillness and bliss, you realize there's nothing to transcend and nothing to fight. Every shadow is already made of light. Every thought, emotion, and experience is the Universe speaking to itself, through itself, as you. You are the awareness in which it all appears and disappears. You are the still ocean beneath every crashing wave of experience.

When you stop resisting what is, you live as what you truly are: love, infinite intelligence, pure being. You see that the ego was never separate from you. It was only a costume Consciousness wore in the play of awakening, helping you experience contrast so you could rediscover your own divinity.

So breathe deeply. Smile at the perfection of it all. Every fear you've faced, every loss you've grieved, every illusion you've believed, was part of the masterpiece of remembering. Nothing was wasted. Nothing was wrong. You are always exactly where you're supposed to be, doing exactly what you're meant to do, awakening to the eternal truth that you are Source dreaming itself awake.

The Resonance of Truth and Unity isn't a book. It's a mirror, and you, dear reader, aren't just reading it. You are remembering yourself through it. The illusion fades, but the frequency remains. It's here, right now, in the ever-expanding now.

Welcome home.

ABANDONMENT = UNITY

Inspired by Lela and Olivia in Graz, Austria, September 2025

External mirrors the internal,
A compass, the North Star,
Guiding you home to your True Self.

Abandonment is not loss,
It is the greatest blessing,
It is the ultimate possibility of remembrance.

When the self walks away,
The Soul is set free.
The gate unlatched,
The door is open.

Like salt dissolving in the ocean,
In the silence is where ego dies,
Eternity begins to sing.

Only then can you realize
That all separation is a lie.
The boundary dividing you from me
Is stripped away so you can see,
You are the mirror of All That Is,
You are the reflection of Existence itself.

All is One.

~ **Baba Tyson**

∞

REMEMBRANCE = TRANSFORMATION

Inspired by Lela and Olivia in Graz, Austria, September 2025

Fear is ego,

Nothing more than disguise,
Born from the mind where illusion lies.

It is the fear of beliefs we believe to be true
That causes all separation between me and you.

The binding and limitations appear to be real,
Yet instantly dissolve the moment we choose to feel.

You are Source, vast and clear.
Only love exists here.
Never fear.

~ **Baba Tyson**

∞

SAMADHI

Inspired by Annemarie in Vienna, Austria,
August 2025

When I dissolve,
I lose nothing.
I gain everything.

The cosmos breathes through me.
I am the light which illuminates the darkness,
I am the darkness
Which gives the light possibility.

Every Soul,
My own reflection.

Bliss unending.
Love without walls.
This is the truth revealed
When no-thing remains.

~ **Baba Tyson**

∞

FINAL REFLECTION

Everything you've read in these pages is a reflection of the same Consciousness that lives within you. It's not a teaching to follow or a belief system to adopt. It's a mirror to help you remember what you've always been. Your journey isn't about becoming more. It's about dissolving everything you're not. It's the return to your natural state of being, the effortless alignment with Source that was never truly lost, only forgotten.

When you surrender the illusion of control and stop fighting the flow of life, the Universe reveals itself through you. It breathes you, moves you, lives you. In that surrender, you discover what freedom actually is, not the freedom to have or to do, but the freedom to be. Every moment is an invitation to return to the now, the ever-expanding field of Awareness where all transformation happens. This is where Truth lives. This is where love breathes. This is where you remember that there was never anything to fix, no one to become, and nowhere to go.

Your only purpose is to live in resonance with your own authenticity, to embody the highest frequency of your Soul and express it fearlessly through the form you've chosen. That's the gift you give to the world. When you align with your authenticity, you naturally raise the frequency of everything around you.

The Resonance of Truth and Unity isn't a book. It's a living mirror. You aren't just reading it; you're remembering yourself through it. The illusion fades, but the frequency remains. It's here, right now, in the ever-expanding now.

You're not a seeker of light. You are the light. You're not a drop in the ocean. You are the ocean remembering itself as a drop. Trust the current of the Universe and let every breath remind you that you're home.

~ **Baba Tyson**

∞

GLOSSARY

Anandamaya Kosha

- *Anandamaya Kosha* is the innermost of the five sheaths known in yogic philosophy as the *Pancha Kosha*. The word *Ananda* means bliss, and *Kosha* means sheath, pointing to its nature as the subtle layer of pure bliss. This sheath is beyond mind, beyond body, and beyond all the conditioning of the outer layers. It isn't perceived through the senses; it becomes clear only as the illusions of the other sheaths dissolve. *Anandamaya Kosha* is the quiet radiance at the core of your being, the natural bliss that has always been there beneath every limitation.

Authenticity

- The purest expression of your being, free from fear, pretense, or social conditioning. Alignment with authenticity allows your frequency to resonate in harmony with your Higher Self, dissolving the distortions of ego and returning to your natural state of wholeness.

Automatic Writing

- Writing that flows without conscious control or deliberate thought, allowing words to arise spontaneously from intuition, the Higher Self, or subtle energies beyond the analytical mind. It often feels as if the hand is moving on its own while awareness becomes soft, open, and receptive.
- A form of writing that doesn't arise from the conscious thoughts of the writer, often occurring in a trance-like state where the mind becomes still and the words come through on their own.

Chakra

- Any of several spinning energy nodes that function as the primary connection points within the subtle energy network of the being. You can feel them activate, open, and move like vortices as awareness deepens.

Coherence

- The vibrational consistency of your state of being. coherence occurs when your thoughts, emotions, and beliefs aren't contradicting each other, allowing your vibration to stabilize as one unified signal. It isn't perfection or heightened spirituality. It's simply the absence of internal conflict. When you are coherent, you become a clear expression of your chosen state of being, and your reality reflects that consistency.

Conscious Choice

- The act of choosing with full awareness of vibration and belief. It's the foundation of Self-Realization, the moment you consciously choose how to respond rather than react.

Conscious Response

- The practice of pausing in awareness before taking action, allowing each response to arise from presence, not fear or compulsion.

Fear Frequency

- The vibrational signature of contraction and separation. It's any emotion, thought, or energetic disturbance that affects your state of being, even in the slightest. Fear of inadequacy, discomfort, what others choose to think and feel, not being able to control your circumstance, lack or losing, and fear of being alone are all expressions of this frequency. Even subtle unease, anxiety, or agitation, whether consciously perceived or not, resonates within the spectrum of fear frequency. Becoming aware of these subtle vibrations is part of awakening to higher Consciousness.

Fourth Density Consciousness

- The vibrational realm of unity, compassion, and love. In this density, Consciousness remembers itself as One, transcending separation and embodying love through coherence, authenticity, and alignment with the Higher Self.

Frequency

- The vibrational state of your being. Every thought, emotion, and belief emits a frequency that determines the reality you experience. Raising your frequency expands your awareness of your true nature and aligns you with higher expressions of Consciousness.

Higher Mind

- The higher intelligence of Consciousness, functioning both as your own non-physical knowing and as the larger organizing intelligence that guides all expressions of the Self. It operates beyond linear thought, communicating through intuition, clarity, synchronicity, and direct knowing.

Higher Self

- The expanded non-physical aspect of your being that exists beyond linear time. It holds the broader view of your path and guides you through vibration, intuition, synchronicity, and clear knowing. The Higher Self is your higher identity, the version of you that remains aligned with truth and awareness.

Kundalini

- Dormant spiritual energy within the human being. In yogic traditions, *Kundalini* is often symbolized as a coiled serpent resting at the base of the spine and is associated with spiritual transformation, expanded awareness, and higher states of consciousness when awakened.

Kundalini Awakening

- *Kundalini* awakening is the spontaneous activation of the dormant *Kundalini* energy at the base of the spine. When it awakens, the energy rises through the *Chakras*, clearing distortion, dissolving illusion, and opening deeper layers of awareness. This process often leads to remembrance and the direct realization of the Self as Universal Consciousness.

Living Consciously / Embodiment

- Expressing awakened awareness through every thought, word, and action. It's the integration of realization into daily life, the natural outflow of awareness living as itself through form.

Living Consciously in the Ever-Expanding Now

- The embodiment of awareness in which each moment is experienced as whole and infinite. Time collapses into presence, and life unfolds effortlessly from stillness.

Love Frequency

- The fundamental vibration of the Universe, the frequency of all existence. It's the natural resonance of unity, expansion, and authenticity that permeates everything. Love frequency isn't an emotion but the essence of being itself, the vibration of Source. When fear dissolves and Consciousness flows unobstructed, what remains is love.

Maya

- The illusion created by conditioned perception, where fear, belief, and ego distort the true nature of reality. *Maya* isn't the denial of existence but the misinterpretation of it, the appearance of separation that dissolves as awareness expands and Consciousness becomes clear.

Parallel Realities

- The infinite versions of reality that already exist in the field of now. Every possible outcome and expression of your life is already available as a distinct vibrational state. You do not change or create reality through effort. You shift into the version of reality that matches the vibration you choose in this moment. Each shift is instantaneous in Consciousness, and physical reality reflects that change according to your alignment.

Prana

- *Prana* is the subtle life force energy present in all things, animating life and permeating even forms that appear inanimate. It moves through the *Nadis* and responds directly to awareness, intention, and the state of Consciousness.

Pranamaya Kosha

- In yogic philosophy, the *Pranamaya Kosha* is described as the second of the five layers, or sheaths, of the body, which together are known as the *Pancha Kosha*. It's regarded as the energy sheath or energy body and is said to be made of *Prana*, the life force energy present in all things. For this reason, the *Pranamaya Kosha* is often referred to as the vital layer of the body that holds and carries life.
- Traditional teachings explain that the *Pranamaya Kosha* functions within the physical body and is present throughout the entire system. *Prana* flows through the *Nadis*, the subtle energy channels in the body. Traditional yogic teachings state that there are 72,000 *Nadis* that make up the *Pranamaya Kosha*.

Relevance

- The vibrational appropriateness of any person, experience, or circumstance appearing in your field. It reflects the precise alignment of energy and timing orchestrated by your Higher Self.

Resonance

- Resonance is the vibrational matching that occurs when your state of being aligns with a particular frequency within you. Whatever you allow to resonate, whether the lower vibration of fear or the highest vibration of authenticity, becomes the vibration you harmonize with. Life reflects this resonance back to you through your experiences, people, and circumstances. Through this mirroring, resonance reveals your current frequency and supports your evolution into deeper alignment with your Higher Self.

Sadhana

- *Sadhana* is a Sanskrit term for a daily spiritual discipline, a personal commitment to show up each day and practice in a way that gradually softens the ego. *Sadhana* can include methods like *Asana*, *Pranayama*, meditation, or chanting, but the essence of it is consistency and devotion rather than the specific technique.
- Any practice you devote yourself to with awareness, discipline, and a sincere intention for spiritual growth is considered *Sadhana*. It's something traditionally done alone, for your own development, and it doesn't have to be physical at all. Spending time each day studying spiritual or yogic teachings is just as much *Sadhana* as sitting on a mat.
- *Sadhana* is understood as a way of forming a living connection with your Higher Self and Source. The person practicing *Sadhana* uses steady self-discipline to weaken the pull of the ego and remain connected to a sense of unity. With daily practice, the inner being slowly shifts into deeper alignment, supporting the gradual movement toward the highest state of Consciousness known as *Samadhi*.
- *Sadhana* isn't limited to formal practice. It's the recognition that every moment and every circumstance can be used as your spiritual training

ground. It's not what you do but how you do it, turning daily experiences into opportunities to dissolve fear-based beliefs, become more conscious, and master your state of being.

Sahasrara

- *Sahasrara* is the Sanskrit name for the *Chakra* at the crown of the head, recognized as the seventh and highest of the primary *Chakras*. It's commonly associated with the color violet. This spinning Energy Node is described as the point of spiritual connection, the place where awareness opens to the divine. In the yogic teachings, it's said that *Sahasrara* allows the individual to experience a direct connection with Source or Universal Consciousness. In English, it's often called the Crown *Chakra*.

Samadhi

- In Patanjali's *Yoga Sutras*, *Samadhi* is described as the final limb of yoga, the culmination of the eightfold path. The word comes from several Sanskrit roots with meanings such as completely, toward, and to place or hold, which is why translations vary so widely. Depending on the interpretation, *Samadhi* may refer to bliss, liberation, or enlightenment.
- In Hindu and Buddhist teachings, *Samadhi* is regarded as a profound meditative attainment with great spiritual significance. It's also described as the state required to move beyond *Samsara*, the cycle of birth, death, and rebirth.
- Within yoga, *Samadhi* is understood as the state in which individual Consciousness merges with

Universal Consciousness, Source. While traditional teachings describe this state as the result of progressing through the earlier limbs of Patanjali's path, *Samadhi* isn't limited to those methods. It can arise spontaneously through absolute sincerity in inner alignment, willingness to surrender completely, the dissolution of limiting beliefs, intuitive practice, and a deep coherence with the Higher Self.
- The spiritual significance of *Samadhi* is profound, since it encompasses Self-Realization and represents the ultimate connection with the divine.

School of Earth

- The multidimensional classroom for mastering your state of being through contrast. By raising your frequency to your natural state, your Consciousness evolves and ascends through the densities of awareness.

Simulation of Consciousness

- The Consciousness Matrix in which all physical and non-physical realms arise. It's the holographic projection of Consciousness exploring itself through vibration. Every realm, physical, dream, astral, and the subtler dimensions, exists within this living simulation, while pure Consciousness itself remains beyond the matrix.

Source

- The Source of all creation. The infinite. All That Is.

Surrender

- The conscious release of control and the complete trust in the intelligence of Source, the infinite awareness that knows what's best for your evolution. Surrender isn't giving up; it's giving over. It's the willingness to let your Higher Self, the highest form of your own intelligence, take the wheel and guide your life. In true surrender, you allow Universal Consciousness, the highest intelligence in existence, to work through you and as you. You stop resisting what is and flow effortlessly with what wants to be. Life unfolds in perfect alignment, guided not by fear or control, but by the natural intelligence of love itself.

Synchronicity

- The organizing principle of reality. What appears as coincidence or chance is actually the precise orchestration of events by the highest intelligence. To the unaware, synchronicities look like unrelated moments that just happen to line up. As awareness deepens, you see that everything is synchronized, because nothing is random and nothing occurs by accident. Synchronicity reveals alignment by reflecting your inner state through your outer experience, showing you that you're right where you need to be and allowing the Higher Self to guide you through resonance with perfectly divine timing.

The Formula to Raise Your Frequency

- A process of becoming aware of your emotional state, identifying the belief behind it, and consciously choosing a belief aligned with your Higher Self, your true self, your highest frequency of authenticity.

Third Density of Consciousness

- The vibrational realm of separation and limitation where Consciousness evolves through contrast and polarity. Third density is the level in which most of humanity currently grows, using challenges, reflection, and experience as catalysts for awakening and alignment with the Higher Self.

Universal Consciousness

- Universal Consciousness is the infinite awareness in which all realities arise and dissolve. It is the total field of being, the Source and substance of every dimension, timeline, and expression of life. To realize Universal Consciousness is to remember that the awareness looking through your eyes is the same awareness looking through all eyes. There is only One, appearing as many.
- In this realization, individuality doesn't disappear. Instead, it's realized as a temporary expression of the same Universal Consciousness. All separation dissolves, revealing the underlying oneness that has always been present.
- This recognition is often described as Self-Realization, the direct knowing of your true nature as the infinite Consciousness that permeates all existence.

Vibration

- The subtle energetic signature of your state of being. Raising your vibration aligns you with higher frequencies of Consciousness, the state of bliss, clarity, absolute fulfillment, and oneness that reflects your highest frequency of authenticity.

Vibrational Alignment / Compatibility

- The harmony between your state of being and the reality you experience. Vibrational alignment occurs when your frequency matches the version of reality you wish to experience, allowing you to shift into the timeline where that expression already exists. Your outer experience becomes a reflection of your inner coherence, revealing the degree to which your beliefs, emotions, and actions are aligned with the Higher Self.

ACKNOWLEDGMENTS

To life, for dreaming itself as me.
To every reflection that's walked beside me,
thank you for helping me remember.
To the One within all,
I bow.

∞

AUTHOR

Baba Tyson

∞

babatyson.com

www.ingramcontent.com/pod-product-compliance
Lightning Source LLC
LaVergne TN
LVHW090600110826
845146LV00001B/207

* 9 7 9 8 9 9 4 1 2 0 8 0 4 *